G000166263

Slide-Tape
and Dual Projection

Slide-Tape and Dual Projection

How to link slide projection with tape recording

RAY BEAUMONT-CRAGGS F.R.P.S.

FOCAL PRESS
London and New York

ISBN 0 240 50748 7

Printed in Great Britain by
STAPLES PRINTERS LIMITED
at The Stanhope Press, Rochester, Kent.

Contents

Introduction

More and more people are discovering the moment of excitement mingled with anxiety which marks the opening of a box of colour slides just returned from development. Only a few years ago, the perfection of these transparencies would have seemed miraculous; but now technical miracles happen every day and are taken for granted. Perhaps photography is becoming too easy, because when that first thrill is over and the pictures have been projected once or twice, interest in them wanes and is soon replaced by boredom.

ADDING SOUND TO PICTURES

The apparent simplicity of taking a photograph is not the principal reason for this rapid discontent. It is due to the fact that our world is increasingly *audio*-visual: sight and sound are constantly linked together in entertainment, instruction, culture and publicity, and we can no longer be satisfied with images alone. Most of us realise this, and when projecting our slides we feel obliged to keep up a flow of commentary which is unfortunately none the better for being improvised. This is certainly no solution. Who would dare to claim that he has never felt himself seized by apprehension when asked point-blank: 'Would you like to see my slides?'

The tape recorder has brought a welcome change to the scene. When the commentary is recorded, it can be well prepared and correctly delivered, stopping at certain moments to give way to appropriate music. This is already a great improvement, but it is just a beginning. Very quickly, the photographer who has added a soundtrack to a selection of his slides finds that he has at his disposal a fascinating medium, which not only enlivens holiday and family records, but offers remarkable possibilities for creative and imaginative presentations. And many tape enthusiasts are bringing a new dimension to their pleasure by combining visuals with their sound recordings.

INTRODUCTION TO SLIDE-TAPE

I can truthfully say that the making and showing of slide-tape features (this ungainly name is the one currently adopted for such productions) now gives me as much satisfaction as film-making, even though the whole of my life has been dominated by a love of cinema. Ever since the age of fourteen, when I filmed my school sports days with a 9·5 Pathé cine camera, I have made movies. Until a few years ago, I had never taken a 35mm colour slide. Apart from an occasional $2\frac{1}{4}$ in. square photograph for family or record purposes, it was movies, movies, all the way.

But one hot summer's day I was lugging my 16mm camera with

its three lenses plus a tripod through one of those country homes of distinction which one can visit, and I suddenly thought: this is absurd. Here I am trying to infuse some sort of life into a basically static subject by all sorts of artifice such as camera movements and framing a waving branch in the foreground, yet I can't even record the inside of the house because there isn't enough light – whereas the simplest and smallest of 35mm still cameras with a slow exposure or a modest flash could record it all in colour!

So I bought a simple and light 35mm camera; I still use it for some of my work. When I had a sufficient number of slides, I felt it would be pleasant to add sound to them, and I discovered that here was a means of expression ideal for certain subjects and moods. It was distinct from cinema, yet akin to it, especially when presented by dual-projection, that is to say with two identical projectors showing the slides alternately. This method, which was developed (or, more precisely, rediscovered) on the Continent, had me so excited that I wrote about it to a celebrated photo magazine, whose editor invited me to demonstrate the process at the 1965 Olympia Photo Fair. Since then I have presented programmes to many societies and clubs on both sides of the Channel.

DEVELOPING THE SUBJECT

This book is the result of my personal experience of slide-tape. It first describes basic technique and the equipment needed to obtain satisfying results with a minimum of complications. Secondly, it develops the numerous possibilities of slide-tape, not only as a means of creative expression but as an aid to education and business.

The final chapters are devoted to new methods of presentation, which enable slides to be shown in more imaginative and spectacular ways. Dual projection is well within the possibilities of the amateur, and has gained prodigious popularity in Europe due to the many visual and rhythmic effects that can be obtained with it. Professional producers of audio-visual spectacles have progressed a stage further, making use of triple and even multi-screen presentations. These are beyond the scope of the lone worker, but not of a group, and some amateur clubs have already produced such slide-tape programmes. However complex the end-product may appear, it is always based on a combination of slides and tape. Only the presentation differs: at first a single projector, then dual projection (essential, in my opinion, for complete enjoyment of the medium of slide-tape), and later, perhaps, more ambitious projects.

The book does not cover colour film processing, because we can leave it confidently to the professional laboratory. There are other publications for those who prefer to process their own slides. Our interest lies more in the aesthetic aspects of colour photography, and we shall deal with its technique only within the limits of our needs. Tape recording, however, is not yet as widespread as photography, so there is rather more about the basic technicalities of sound.

HOW SLIDE-TAPE STARTED

Slide-tape is much more than just a matter of equipment and technique, and I have tried to balance these practical questions with more general aspects, together with a little historical background. The origins of this form of spectacle can be traced a long way back, and are both curious and interesting. For example, is it not extraordinary that in Paris at the time known as the Terror, the most fearful period of the French Revolution, a man who called himself Robertson was presenting slide projections with sound accompaniment in the ruins of a convent only a few yards from the spot where Louis XVI was guillotined? As though there were not enough horror in the streets, his entertainments, which drew large crowds, were nightmarish evocations of spectres, skeletons and other ghastly apparitions. Most striking of all, perhaps, is the modern-sounding name this talented showman gave to the magic lantern he had designed to produce his effects: he called it a Fantascope.

This was taking place a century before the first (silent) performance of the Cinematograph in 1895. And during the years preceding that event, hundreds of quite complex programmes of projection were being given throughout Britain, the Continent and the United States. It is as well to remember that slide presentations have a long and distinguished history, if only to counter the attacks of those moviemaking purists who deride them as 'the poor man's cinema'. Certainly it costs far less to produce a slide-tape feature than a movie of equivalent length filmed on the smallest gauge; but this should not be the main argument in favour of slides. It is obvious that whenever movement, action and a direct explanation of a story are essential, the motion picture is irreplaceable; but slide-tape is a different means of expression, well suited to certain types of subject which are unlikely to be equally satisfactory if recorded on cine film.

A NEW ART FORM

Any new art form has to develop its own rules and language even though it borrows from another. Ever since photography was invented it has fought a battle with painting: in order to get away from 'mechanical reproduction', painters turned to abstraction; today photographers have followed suit. Before finding its own direction, cinema was merely filmed theatre; now the electronic camera of television is bringing a new concept of visual art.

The medium of colour slides with sound is a recent development which has made great strides but can still be considered experimental. Its expansion is due to the increasing popularity of the 35mm camera, but the dynamism of its presentation comes from a technique more allied to cinema than to the projection of lantern-slides. Is it photography? Is it cinema? A 'link' between the two? Frankly, I neither know nor care, for such considerations are to me just futile hair-splitting.

All I do know is that I love both cinema and photography, and that my aim is to open wide to others the doors of this world that I treasure. A world in which all can participate together in the glory of colour, the wonder of sound, freely interpreted, in the manner that suits us best.

Essential Equipment

Slide-tape can be very simple, yet even in its most elementary form it is satisfying and entertaining. It makes use of equipment that many people already own. The basic difference between the usual home slide show and the presentation which, for want of a better name, we shall have to call a 'slide-tape feature' is that in the former, the transparencies are often projected in a happy-go-lucky manner with an improvised commentary that ambles on until there are no more pictures to show or until the spectators have dropped off to sleep, whereas the feature is a carefully planned short production, consisting of a limited number of slides arranged in sequences, combined with a tape recording that includes narration, music and possibly sound effects.

In its most advanced and creative form, slide-tape makes use of two linked projectors, a method now adopted all over the world for important shows in view of the smoothness and impact it adds to the presentation, and the possibilities it offers for certain remarkable visual transitions.

But whether the result is to be complex or simple, the essential equipment is the same: a camera, a tape recorder, a projector, and – as some musical accompaniment is usually necessary – a record player when making the sound track.

CHOOSING THE CAMERA

Nowadays nearly every camera is suitable for taking colour slides. From the inexpensive instant-load cartridge variety to the most gadget-laden reflex, the choice is limited only by personal taste and the amount you are prepared to pay. As far as exposure of the film is concerned, a simple camera will do as well as a more complicated one in the majority of cases: that is to say when there is sufficient light. 'Fast' lenses and 'slow' shutter speeds come into their own only when conditions are bad.

Of course, the lens of a camera costing only a few pounds cannot be expected to give the pinpoint sharpness of a high-quality type, but for the small home screen it may be quite satisfactory. Its principal inconvenience is that it is usually not interchangeable. In black and white photography it is possible to crop a negative by enlarging certain portions of it; but with colour transparencies there is little that can be done to alter the composition of the image once it has been taken. It is therefore important to be able to shoot exactly what is wanted, and for this a choice of lenses of different focal length is desirable. On a 35mm camera, apart from the normal lens of 50 or 55mm, it is usual to consider a moderately wide-angle of 35mm and a long-focus type of 90 or 135mm. Converters that double the focal length are convenient to carry and inexpensive. The results may not be quite as sharp as those obtained with a regular lens – especially at the corners of the image – but this defect is sometimes less noticeable on a projected picture than on a print.

Very big close-ups are fascinating in colour, and the impact of a tiny object enlarged on a screen is considerable. The single-lens reflex is the ideal camera for this type of work, apart from which it is very helpful to be able to gauge accurately the area covered by the lens, when photographing titles, for instance. It could be said that the reflex camera, by giving a clear impression of depth of field, provides a special style of picture-making all its own. But it has one major disadvantage (apart from its price): its bulk, which makes it very far from being a pocketable camera.

For the great majority of slide-tape productions, 35mm has become the standard film size. This does not mean that for your personal pleasure – or even in the aids to education and work study that will be mentioned later – you cannot use 126 instant-load cartridges, half-frame, or any size you fancy; but it does mean that if you should become keen enough on the medium to wish to enter a competition, it is very likely that it will be limited to that format. For certain large-scale programmes on giant screens, 6×6 cm transparencies are used. The results are superb; but the cost of the film and especially the limited amount of projection equipment available in this size, make such presentations exceptional.

CHOOSING THE TAPE RECORDER

Whereas the choice of a camera is governed mainly by personal considerations, your selection of the tape recorder must be guided by some specific factors. There is now a great variety of recorders, some with features that may be useful in one field – such as language study – but having little point in other work.

The main point to bear in mind is that the *quality* of the sound is vital to the success of a slide-tape presentation. The lack of movement of the image, and the fact that there is time to study it, might imply that the photography should be better than that of a motion-picture, but this is not strictly true: the soundtrack is even more important. It is difficult to concentrate on two things at once, and when watching a film, aural standards are not too critical; but with a suspended, still image, bad sound is very noticeable and the photographer should certainly go for the greatest fidelity he can achieve. Unfortunately there are no short cuts with regard to cost. If you buy cheap material, you must accept the limitations involved, or at least be prepared to have to change to more sophisticated equipment later, when finances permit.

There are two basic types of recorder: portable (battery operated) and transportable (mains), the former usually being smaller and lighter. (It is possible to purchase a tape deck without amplifiers or speakers, for incorporation into an audio set-up. In this case a pre-amplifier is necessary in order to boost the level of the signal to the power amplifier.) For on-the-spot recording where a mains supply is not available or space is limited, the portable (and in particular the popular cassette model) is a useful accessory. But, as we have noted that the highest quality is required, a mains unit is essential, because not only can bigger and more powerful components be included in it, but larger reels and higher recording speeds – which would quickly exhaust batteries – can be used.

TAPE SPEEDS

A few years ago, the speed of 7½ in. per sec. was considered necessary for good reproduction, particularly of music, and some contests still insist on it. But today the improvement in technique is such that the most usual speed is 3¾ ips, which is available on nearly every recorder. However, the faster speed makes editing of the tape easier. If you should make cuts and splices in the recording it is wise to re-record the result on to a final uncut tape; in this case the original should be made at 7½ ips and the copy can be taken at 3¾ ips. Some recorders have a third speed of 1⅞ ips which is intended to record speech and is used for economy and not quality. A fourth speed of 15 ips, found on some machines, is for professional work of exceptionally high standard beyond the scope of our needs.

MONO OR STEREO?

As far as the reproduction of the final track is concerned, the answer is mono. Stereophonic sound adds little to the average slide show and can even be slightly ridiculous in the context of a home performance. It only comes into its own in large-scale spectaculars using very wide or multiple screens; but we haven't reached that stage yet! So we could say that any machine capable of giving good sound will do. But as you may eventually wish to make recordings that incorporate certain effects as well as voice and music, note that a stereo recorder, used monaurally, offers many interesting possibilities. There are two separate amplifiers for playback, with independent control over each, and if it is possible to record on one track while playing back the other, a cue commentary can be heard while the sound-track proper is being made. Or, by using the tracks separately, the commentary can be recorded on one and the music and effects on the other in perfect synchronization; either can be partially erased and re-recorded without the other being affected. And when they are replayed together, they may be easily balanced so that the volume of one does not overpower the other.

Half-track stereo recorders offer splendid sound quality but are expensive and mainly used by professionals. Half-track mono gives good sound too, but means that only simple recordings can be made. The quality of quarter-track is theoretically inferior, but it is still extremely good, and as the actual level of recording plays a part in quality, it is worth remembering that in stereo equipment the output power levels are given per channel, therefore the volume of sound available for a given figure will be more than that from a monaural recorder.

OUTPUTS

Anything below 2 W of output power is useless for a show. Between 3 and 5 W is sufficient for the home, and even allows a little volume in reserve, which is always a good idea.

The sound should preferably come from the direction of the screen, but as the producer of the slide feature is usually also its projectionist, this causes him difficulty if the tape recorder is on the other side of the room. Of course, as it is the track that governs the passage of the pictures, in productions that are not mechanically synchronized it is possible to ask a friend to push the button on the recorder when you are ready to begin, but this is not a very elegant system. Also it is preferable to have the machine at hand to be able to vary the volume or tone controls during the show. So make sure that the recorder has external loudspeaker sockets for a remote speaker by the screen. Nowadays nearly all recorders are fitted with them, but check anyway if only to find the type of plug required for the connection. There is an irritating and quite incredible lack of standardization of plugs, each manufacturer seeming to take a fiendish delight in using a different shape.

MICROPHONE

The type of microphone is important; certain voices seem to change their personality according to the microphone used. The cheap crystal microphone is really not good enough, and has the added disadvantage of being usable only with a very short lead. Like lenses, microphones have a 'taking angle'. The wide-angle type records from all directions, which may be useful for a crowd scene but makes the taping of a commentary difficult by picking up all sorts of unwanted background noises. For this purpose, a narrow-angle directional microphone is best.

RECORDING LEVEL INDICATORS

Fully automatic recording level control, available on more expensive machines, permits the signal to be governed by electronic circuits within fixed limits. Other recorders have a meter for setting the recording level, often a neon tube known as a 'magic eye'. More accurate and practical is the needle moving over a graduated dial: in the case of stereo, there should be one dial per channel.

PAUSE KEY

This is a very useful accessory, enabling the recording to be stopped and restarted without any 'clonking' sound on the tape. Some older models have to be held in place by finger pressure; the more recent permanent type which, once set, stays put until depressed again is perhaps easier to control, but this is a matter of opinion.

MAGNETIC TAPE

Recording tape is made in various thicknesses, the thinner types allowing more tape and thus longer recording on a given size of reel. Tapes are usually classified as follows:
Standard: This, the original type, has been replaced in most cases by the long-playing variety, which is acoustically similar but is more supple and adheres more closely to the magnetic heads.
Long Play: Is now universally employed for both 2- and 4-track recordings, especially on machines having three heads (erase, and separate record and playback).
Double Play: Can be recommended for use on combined heads (i.e. the same one for both recording and playback), as this type of recorder works best with thin and very supple tapes giving good contact.
Triple Play: Is intended for combined heads, slow recording speeds, and small reels. The reduced thickness of the base is compensated by a greater density of the magnetic coating.

As very few recorders used by amateurs have separate recording and playback heads, the most popular tape is the double play. This gives more than adequate length of playing time for most slide-tape features. If, however, your machine takes only small reels and you are making an unusually long production, then you can always fall back on triple play.

The letters L H (Low noise, High output) apply to tapes used for very hi-fi recordings on top-quality recorders.

RECORD PLAYER

The record player should be of good quality, and must of course be fed into the tape recorder through one of the plugs intended for that purpose. Satisfactory results cannot be obtained by recording the sound emerging from the speaker of the player via a microphone. The tape recording of a disc should be as perfect as possible, without hum and with normal base and treble response.

TYPES OF PROJECTOR

For a start, just about any slide projector will do, on condition that it has at least a semi-automatic slide-changing device, as you will no doubt prefer not to be feeding the transparencies in one by one while following the sound-track. 'Stack-loading', available on some projectors, is one solution, but can be prone to jamming. More usual are the conventional magazines.

One inconvenience to be considered with these is that they hold only 36 or 50 slides and as there will be times when you wish to present them in quick rhythmic succession, they will soon be used up and the magazine will have to be changed after about five minutes, that is at least once and possibly twice during the course of each production. This can be very disturbing for the audience if it is not slickly done, and calamitous for the operator if he cannot catch up with the sound track. With dual projection using two identical machines this is naturally less of a problem, as 100 slides generally cover all but the longest slide-tape features. (I have always made them do so, as I refuse to take the risk of a change-over during the show!)

For single-projector presentation, a quiet revolution has been taking place with the introduction of the rotary type machine, sometimes known as the Jumbo. Some of these circular magazines take 80 slides, others up to 120, and the usual principle is that they slot into the normal channel, jutting up into the air like a ferris wheel (there is one notable exception whose tray is horizontal). As each transparency is removed, the changing mechanism causes the magazine to revolve just enough to bring the next one into position. Normal straight slide magazines can also be used with the 'vertical' projectors.

Most slide projectors have a wide-angle lens, which is all right at home, as the extra sharpness and luminosity of transparencies compared with cinema deserves as large a screen as possible. But for public shows, such a lens necessitates either a gigantic screen (and a powerful light) or placing the projector among the audience, which is not only poor showmanship but usually means tilting up the machine, resulting in a 'keystone' effect. If possible, a longer focal length lens should be used; so if you are thinking of going beyond the home circle, find out whether other lenses than the standard one are available.

Equipment for dual projection is of several different types, and is dealt with in pages 114–126.

AUTOMATIC SLIDE-CHANGE

Fully automatic slide changing controlled by a push button is fine, but make sure that the mechanism accepts the extra thickness of glass mounts easily and also that it moves at a fairly rapid rate. Certain machines are maddeningly ponderous in their movements and bring you close to a nervous breakdown if you are trying to present a fast-moving sequence. Some models now have a built-in timing switch that can be set to change the transparencies automatically at specified intervals of from 4 to 30 sec. This may be of use in rare circumstances (a display in a shop window, for instance) but apart from that, the very idea is an abomination. This system cannot in any way replace a synchronizer, because the timing must vary from slide to slide.

SYNCHRONIZED SLIDE CHANGING

In recent years I have presented many programmes of dual-projected slide-tape features in such hallowed haunts as the Royal Society of Arts, the Olympia Photo Fair and the Société Française de Photographie; I have never yet used a synchronizer. This is not to say that the device is a bad thing to have; but as I do the projecting myself and know by heart the places at which the change-overs should be made, it is just one more item to be set up and possibly to go wrong. Most people prefer to have some sort of a signalling system, though, especially if they don't show their productions often, for the timing is soon forgotten.

The simplest method is to stick patches of metallic foil on the shiny side of the tape at every point where a change of slide is to take place. The tape is run past two small contacts mounted on the recorder, so that the foil makes and breaks any circuit connected to them. If the projector is manually operated, this device can be designed to give a visual signal by being connected to a small battery and bulb which will light up at each mark. An automatic projector with a remote-control lead can be connected directly to the contacts so that the slides change themselves. The method is cheap and within the scope of anyone who likes a little electrical do-it-yourself, but is far from ideal. Sticking patches on tapes is a messy business, and as the tape is made thicker at those points and less flexible, this may have a momentary effect on the sound, or at worst jam in the recorder. Far better (and, as usual, more expensive) is the pulse synchronizer.

PULSE SYNCHRONIZERS

Several excellent makes of pulse synchronizer are now available. In effect, these devices are small, simplified tape recorders made to be placed alongside the main recorder near its take-up spool. Some units are light and have to be attached to it, but others are substantially made and quite heavy, and can stand on their own. The head of the synchronizer is lined up level with the tape path; the recorder should therefore have a flush deck, although it is possible to cut slots in the side of models with sunk decks. The tape is looped around the synchronizer head so as to run from the recorder's capstan through the synchronizer and on to the take-up spool.

The unit implants a pulse on to the bottom quarter track of either a twin or four-track tape when the appropriate button is pressed, so that stereo recordings can still be made on four-track machines. If an automatic projector is connected up at the same time, the slide will change simultaneously, so a check can be kept on both sound and picture while they are being synchronized. If you should make a mistake and record a pulse in the wrong place it doesn't matter, for you need only rewind the tape a few turns, play it back to the last correct pulse, then push the 'record' button and carry on. The incorrect pulse will be erased, as on a normal recorder.

One final point: make sure the plugs connecting projector and synchronizer are compatible, for here again there seems to be no standardization.

Taking the Picture

Although it is convenient to regard slide-tape as a link between still photography and the motion picture, this can be a rather negative way of thinking. Slide-tape is not just 'cinema without the action', even less a poor relation. In one respect, at least, it is positively ahead: the quality of the images. They may not move, but they have a superb clarity and sharpness superior to the best 16mm movies. And as these are *photographs,* taken individually, all the techniques of the still camera can be employed. At its simplest, this means shots taken in conditions impossible for the cine camera: time exposure or flash. If you are an expert, it could mean solarization, negative colour, diffusion, distortion, infra-red. These techniques must not be used as an end in themselves, but they offer possibilities leading to a personal photographic style.

FILMS AND FILTERS

There are many makes of colour film on the market. All give excellent results, but as obviously no combination of dyes can reproduce the colours of Nature with absolute precision, each brand of film has its own special tendencies: in this one the overall cast is a little blue, in that one the skin tones are more pink, the other has more contrast. The widest selection lies in the slow-to-medium range of sensitivity, where a fairly strong light is required; the make that you choose will be a question of personal taste. In the case of 'high-speed' emulsions, the choice is more limited. In bright sunshine the faster films are too sensitive for the simpler type of camera, because they are intended for use with rapid shutter speeds or in poor lighting conditions. A slight loss of fine detail and colour accuracy must be accepted in exchange for this extra sensitivity.

In black and white, the same film can be used without filtering both in daylight or by artificial light, but this is not possible with colour stock. The human eye is remarkably adaptable and makes adjustments for the different quality of the illumination, but a photographic emulsion cannot do this. If it is 'balanced' for daylight, all shots taken on it by tungsten light (i.e. electric bulbs) have an orange hue. To counteract this, special artificial-light type film is manufactured with a different colour response. The problem when using 35mm is that a cassette contains 20 or even 36 exposures, and you may have to take pictures both by day and by night on the same roll. So a decision will have to be taken as to the type of film you will use, bearing in mind that it is possible to alter the rendering of each by the use of tinted filters.

A solution to this question is the one adopted for Super-8 movies. The only filmstock available in this format is of artificial-light type, but the cameras have a built-in correction filter for daylight which swings out of the way when a flood-lamp is plugged into them. Long before Super-8 was thought of, many film-makers working with Standard-8 or 16mm made use of the same principle if they shot a good deal of film indoors, because the Type A film was more sensitive than the daylight stock. With a pink filter outdoors it was the same speed as the daylight type which, on the other hand, became very slow when used by artificial light with a correcting blue filter.

This sounds a good idea, and some people have adopted it for their slides. But there is one major snag: the actual filter to be used. In the Super-8 camera, this is relatively small and incorporated behind the lens; on a still camera the filter is considerably larger and must be placed on the front, and perhaps changed from one lens to another. The glass must be of excellent quality, for what would be the point of buying a first-class lens, and then distorting the result by shooting through a 'bottle-bottom'?

In any case, much indoor photography is taken with electronic flash or blue bulbs, balanced for use with daylight film; and it would be a pity not to be able to take advantage of the extremely fast daylight-type colour films now available. So I would say that in the majority of cases, artificial-light type film is unnecessary. And oddly enough, even for outdoor night photography by available light, many people find that its cold and sometimes greenish hue is less to their taste than the warm golden tone that 'daylight' films give to subjects such as floodlit buildings.

NIGHT PHOTOGRAPHY BY AVAILABLE LIGHT

One of the major advantages of slides over cinema is the comparative ease with which good results can be obtained at night with the minimum of equipment. So let us make the most of this opportunity of taking some really interesting pictures in unusual lighting situations. With sensitive film and a fast lens it is possible to hand-hold the camera, but for most subjects a tripod is needed, as well as a cable release and a lens hood, the latter not only to shield the lens from extraneous light but also to protect it from the weather, as many fine night shots are made in rain and snow.

Lighted streets, shop windows, floodlit buildings, neon signs, funfairs and fireworks all provide a variety of excellent material, and with a little experience are not much more difficult to take than daylight scenes. The only subject that is just about impossible to photograph at night is the general scenic view or landscape.

Nearly all so-called 'night' shots of landscapes or buildings are in fact taken at twilight, when there is still a glow in the sky against which the horizon, houses and trees stand out in silhouette. The exact moment needs careful calculation, as it must be bright enough for a short time exposure yet be after lighting-up. With cameras other than 35mm, a popular method is to make two exposures on the same piece of film, one just after the sun has disappeared and another an hour or so later when the lights are all on. Of course the camera must be on a very solid tripod and not move between the two shots, and the double-exposure prevention device renders such simple trickery very complex. As both exposures will be of over a second it is theoretically possible to set the shutter open on the B setting and cover and uncover the lens by means of the lens-cap (if it is quite opaque), but it has to be put on and off with great care so as not to change the position of the camera.

The actual exposure can be found only by trial and error, and depends on the amount of detail required in the darker parts of the picture. Excessive exposure can give the impression that the photograph was taken in daylight. An average basis for experiment is 5 sec at *f*5·6 on a 50–64 ASA film.

Open landscapes can be photographed by 30 min or more exposure under a full moon, but the best way is to cheat, as is regularly done in movies. The scene, underexposed by one or two stops, is shot through a blue-green filter in strong sunlight with plenty of harsh shadows. If preferred, artificial-light type colour film may be used *without* its correction filter for daylight. This gives a cold blue rendering. If figures are to be included, they can be taken in semi-silhouette by shooting against the light, but from a fairly high angle to eliminate the sky, which would be very pale and spoil the effect.

LIGHTED STREETS AND SHOP WINDOWS

Even in black and white, ancient lamp-lit courtyards, alleyways and street corners make fine pictures, and in colour they can be even more delightful. Their overall neutral tones are occasionally highlighted by a tint of green from a tree, or a red or blue beam from a curtained window. Some old towns still have cobbled pavements, and these are extremely photogenic, especially when wet. Rain is of great help at night, adding interesting reflections and increasing the available light, thus permitting shorter exposures. Snow, haze and even fog give a touch of mystery and romance, transforming the most hideous of modern constructions into things of beauty.

The more important public monuments are usually quite brightly floodlit and a brief time exposure is sufficient. The only problem here is that the result may be flat and dead-looking unless some sort of foreground is included, such as trees, foliage or another building.

Shop windows also have plenty of light. As a rule it is provided by floodlamps, but if neon tubes are included the colour problem becomes tricky because the floods normally require artificial-light type for correct rendering, whereas fluorescent lighting may be better on daylight film (although results are unpredictable with this illumination). Fortunately, precise colour rarely matters in this case, and an 'off-beat' mixture may even add a novel touch. Apart from the display itself, interesting pictures may be obtained of people looking at it. Highly recommended in this category are small children outside toyshops at Christmas time. They are intent on what they are looking at, and may be still enough for exposures of 1 or 2 sec to be attempted.

NEON SIGNS, FUNFAIRS AND FIREWORKS

Some displays of neon advertising are so bright that they require an exposure of only 1/30 or 1/60 sec even on slow film, but care must be taken to photograph them from close range so that they fill the frame, as no detail of the building around them will be recorded with such a short exposure. Funfairs include so many different types of lighting that every sort of technique can be employed. The stalls are similar to shop windows in that the participants may be the subject of the picture or merely silhouettes in the foreground. There is so much colour around that it is tempting to use flash to give bright results, but the gain in sharpness and vivid hues cannot make up for the lack of 'atmosphere'.

The merry-go-rounds and other large mechanical revolving machines produce pleasant abstract patterns and streaks of colour when photographed with a long time exposure. Black backgrounds enable various interesting effects of double images to be obtained when the transparencies are presented by dual-projection (see page 134) if the principal subject is composed so as to appear in the dark area of the preceding slide. Night shots are obviously ideal for this.

A curious French production shown at one Vichy Festival consisted entirely of time exposures of neon signs and city streets at night, interspersed with close-ups of a woman photographed with strong backlighting against a black background. Her man had left her, and she was 'drinking to forget'. As the (fortunately short) story unfolded, the outdoor night scenes, which were clear and sharp at the start, having been taken on a firm support, became more and more streaky as the tripod was abandoned. Then the camera was at first held as firmly as possible so that the lights were only slightly blurred, but jerked in a zig-zag movement for later shots. The portraits of the heroine that mixed in and out were lit in an increasingly eccentric manner with coloured gelatines before the lamps.

Time exposures are also usually necessary for fireworks. Instantaneous shutter-speeds may suffice for small luminous set-pieces but will give disappointing results with rockets which, even when taken at the peak moment of the burst, usually end up on a slide looking like diminutive spiders in a sea of ink. The recognized and best method is to set the camera on a tripod pointing in the general direction of the display and open the lens while keeping it masked by a piece of black card. As the rocket is fired, the lens is unmasked and left open during the entire trajectory. The most spectacular results are obtained by repeating the operation two or three times on the same film-frame by leaving the lens open, masking it between firings, and unmasking as soon as the rocket takes off. Then the 'flowers in the sky' are transformed into a bouquet.

FLOWERS

With colour film in the camera you will naturally take many close-ups of flowers. Apart from babies and furry animals, no subject guarantees such instant success – so much so that it can suffice alone as a theme for a feature. Taking a general view of a garden is no different from other types of outdoor photography, but capturing the ephemeral beauty of a single bloom is not easy, and requires patience and careful preparation. The main problems are movement, lighting, and background.

In extreme close-shots of very small flowers, their movement can be almost as difficult to stop as that of a fast car. A breath of wind or a tremor from a passing vehicle can set them swaying, and fast shutter speeds are needed for sharp results. But increasing the shutter speed means opening up the lens, and that in turn reduces the depth of field, already minimal at such short range. So in many cases it is necessary to use high-speed film.

Strong sunlight makes for bright colours but produces high contrast and black shadows. A piece of white card (or a handkerchief) can be held or fixed to one side to reflect light into the dark areas; but the best light is slightly diffused sun. Blooms with simple outlines and interesting patterns and tints should be lighted from the front; those with ragged edges or translucent petals look better backlit against a dark background. On a dull day, electronic flash can be used as an artificial sun.

The colour rendering varies according to the source of illumination, the time of day and also the type of film. All emulsions have difficulty in recording blue flowers, gentian being rendered pink and bluebells, mauve. The reason for this is said to be that they radiate infra-red rays to keep cool, and these rays give a reddish cast to the film. Whatever the explanation, there is little that can be done about it.

Something can and must be done about backgrounds, however. A shot of a flower may be ruined by a conflicting highlight behind it or by an out-of-focus but just recognizable fence. Tall flowers like hollyhocks can be easily taken against the sky, but small plants must be separated from their surroundings. The usual method is to fasten a large piece of card (or a roll of special paper) between sharpened stakes pushed into the ground. Placed in a bow shape, this also protects the flower from the wind.

Deep-toned blooms show up well against a ground of pale hue, but the opposite is more striking, and with a very dark background dual-projection effects (see page 134) can be used. A whole series of shots taken against a blank, featureless background, however, will at length seem artificial, and more variety should be attempted. An out-of-focus lawn in shadow is very good; to obtain this background or others that seem suitable it may be necessary to cheat by cutting the flower and photographing it away from the plant. It can be tied – or fixed with cellulose tape – to a stick, and set up where the light is appropriate.

CLOSE-UPS

The focusing range of most slide cameras being from infinity down to 2 or 3 ft, attachments are necessary when it is desired to photograph subjects closer than this. Focusing is very critical at short range, so a reflex camera is the most practical for close-up work. If the lens is interchangeable, extension tubes or a bellows unit are placed between it and the camera body. The former are less expensive but provide only a fixed set of distances (which can be varied a little in conjunction with the normal focusing movement of the lens), whereas the bellows unit is continuously adjustable and can also be extended further than the tubes to give greater reproduction ratios.

When the camera extension is increased by tubes or bellows, extra exposure is necessary, the lens aperture being opened up in proportion to the longer lens-film distance. The normally-indicated exposure is therefore multiplied by a correction factor which is obtained by dividing the focal length of the lens into the total extension (i.e. focal length plus length of extension tubes or bellows). Thus, if you use a 50mm lens and a 25mm extension tube or bellows extension, the factor is 75/50=1½.

The increase is very rapid as the lens approaches the subject, passing from a barely noticeable half-stop at about eighteen inches away (and many lenses focus that close without added extension) to a full two stops (× 4) for a same-size reproduction (1 : 1). Extension tubes and bellows units are usually provided with a chart of exposure tables adapted to their particular requirements. With through-the-lens metering they can be disregarded, because the integral meter reads the exposure not only through the lens but also through whatever accessories are being used and makes automatic compensation, so no further adjustments are necessary.

Close-ups may be taken with simple viewfinder cameras (or reflex cameras whose lens is not removable) by adding a supplementary lens clipped or screwed to the front like a filter. This requires no increase in exposure, but if it is composed of a simple uncorrected element of the spectacle lens type it can degrade the performance of the camera lens which must be stopped well down if definition is to be maintained to the corners of the picture.

When the camera lens is set at infinity, the supplementary lens focuses it on objects at a distance equal to the focal length of the supplementary lens. A 50 cm supplementary lens added to any camera lens focused on infinity will focus the camera on objects 50 cm (approx. 20 in.) in front of it. At this distance, the normal lens of a 35mm camera will cover an area of about 7 in. × 11 in. When a non-reflex camera approaches as close as this to the subject, its lens no longer covers exactly the same areas as its viewfinder, and focusing is critical enough to need accurate measurement with a ruler. Both these problems can be solved by a simple and easily-made gadget.

HOME-MADE FRAMING DEVICE

The device consists of a wire frame very slightly larger than the area taken in by the camera (with its close-up attachment), held at the correct distance either by stiff wires fixed to a ring or cardboard tube around the lens mount (this looks rather like a lampshade frame, must be very light so as not to cause damage, and may hide the aperture and shutter settings) or else by a thin narrow strip of plywood attached to the underside of a small wooden box which in turn is screwed into the tripod bush of the camera. Another bush will have to be made under the plywood strip to hold the device plus the camera on the tripod.

To discover the exact distance at which the frame must be set and the area it will cover, draw a series of intersecting black lines with a felt pen on a piece of white card, and set the card up on a wall of a darkened room, with a strong light projected on it. Place the supplementary lens on the camera, open the shutter, open the back of the camera and hold a small piece of tracing paper in the position normally occupied by the film. Move the camera towards and away from the card until the black lines appear at their sharpest on the image seen on the tracing paper. Mark on the card the extreme limits of this image and note the distance and position of the camera relative to the card.

This gadget is very useful when photographing not only flowers but all sorts of small subjects that need to be carefully lined up. You will find it particularly useful when reproducing your titles.

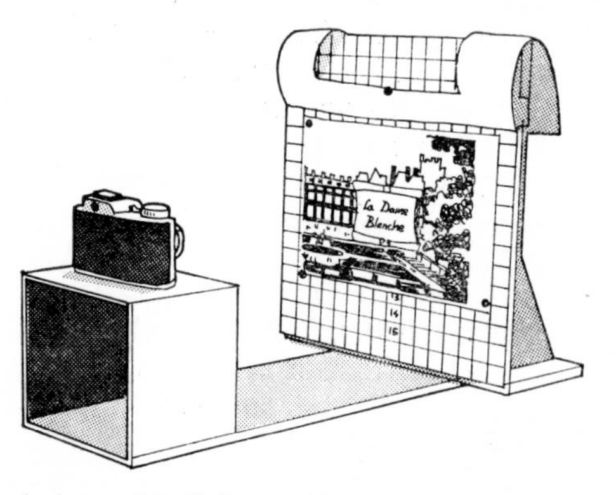

Simple wooden device used for lining up titles with a non-reflex camera.

TITLES

Are titles necessary? I certainly think so. Just as a book needs a title-page, so a slide-tape feature is incomplete without that important element of presentation. I naturally do not mean that you should fall into the absurd trap of copying the unending lists beloved of TV and motion-picture producers; one slide bearing the name of the feature preceded by a simple *John Smith presents* is usually more than adequate, although you can name the narrator and eventually the hero and heroine if they have played an important part. Your modesty may prefer merely a main and an *End* title, with no personal names at all; the length of the production will naturally influence you. For example, a visual interpretation of a musical composition or song lasting three minutes would be somewhat of a comedown after a two-minute introduction.

For a mediaeval evocation, a title based on illuminated MS of the period.

The presentation of professional films shows great imagination nowadays, and you can certainly gain inspiration from them. The actual lettering, background and colour should be in character with the atmosphere to be created. Until recently the amateur found it very difficult to produce well-written titles and usually made use of cut-out felt, cork or plaster letters, which have the disadvantage of looking rather coarse, of being large and so requiring oversize

Lettering adapted to the style of a 16th-Century engraving.

backgrounds if they are not to be very cramped, and of being available only in limited stock styles. In order to avoid using them, there was always the pleasant variation (still valid today) of writing in the sand of a beach, in snow, or on a misty window, using pebbles or flower petals, carving it in wood or just scribbling in chalk on a wall, according to the theme invoked. Also, ready-made titles can sometimes be found, such as the cover of a book or a travel brochure.

Instant rub-off letters now make it possible for everyone to create professional-looking titles. Originally black, they exist today in white and in colours, in various styles, and they can be applied to many types of background including glass.

The actual measurements of this background depend on the size of the letters available and also on the possibilities of the camera with which the title is to be photographed. If the camera is used with a supplementary lens focusing only at a fixed distance, the title will naturally have to conform to the area covered by the lens at that particular distance. The little wire frame gadget described above is of help in this instance. With a reflex camera and a full range of extension tubes or bellows, any size of layout can be taken.

The most usual measurements for title cards are between 8 in. × 6 in. and 10 in. × 12 in. (with a 35mm image, the proportions are more precisely 7 in. × 10½ in.). Do not skimp on the card; it is imperative to leave good, full margins all around the lettering. With slide-tape the wording will usually be very brief, consisting of the main title, perhaps a credit or two, and an 'end'. But if for some special reason you should decide to include an explanatory sub-title, remember that very often two short titles are more effective and pleasing to read than one long one. And the old rule of Mack Sennett days still holds good in most cases: never more than seven words in a title unless the extra words are really vital.

I have seen very good slide-series that started off in a slap-dash manner with a title typed on to a piece of tracing-paper and placed directly in a mount: this is really treating the audience lightly, and it will feel a little uncomfortable even if what follows is first-class. There is also the opposite style: superb lettering accompanied by stentorian music played by a vast orchestra, announcing an insipid collection of views. Here, discomfort will be replaced by irritation, because the promise has not been kept.

PHOTOGRAPHING TITLES

When photographing a title, the most important point to watch is the lining up of the camera. The title card must be parallel to the film-plane, that is to the back of the camera. If it is not, a 'keystone'

For a history of Napoleon, the jacket of an old book

effect is obtained and, at close range, the image may not be perfectly sharp from side to side. In cine work, a cross-shaped wooden or metal device known as a titler is often used. The camera is screwed to one end, facing an upright support in which the title card is placed. Light bulbs in reflectors are fixed at each end of the crossbar, to provide even illumination when artificial light is employed.

This structure enables rapid lining up and provides the firm

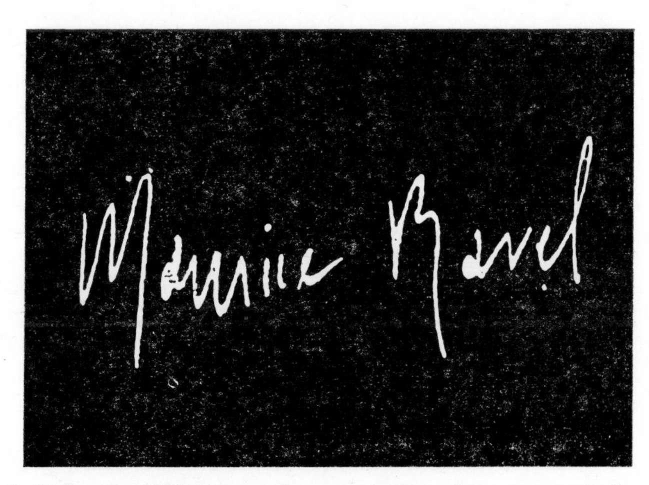

For the biography of Maurice Ravel, a reproduction of the composer's signature.

support essential to movie making, but is not really necessary when a photograph is to be taken. It is usually sufficient to pin the title card to a board and place the board on an easel, or if no easel is available, on a chair. The camera, on its tripod, is then carefully lined up.

A title need not always be considered as similar to a drawing or painting that must be accurately copied; in some cases it can be looked on as a subject for varied lighting effects, particularly if the background is light-toned or in a plain colour. For example, the larger plaster or felt letters will cast shadows if the sun is shining and the board is angled sideways to the light. This can be attractive, and the same result is obtained in artificial light by putting a photoflood or spotlight very low and fairly close to the title; the part of the title nearest to the lamp will be lighter than the rest, but this, too, may be agreeable. For romantic effects, shadows can be cast on the card by placing branches or patterned screens in front of a single source of light.

LIGHTING THE TITLE

It is of course more usual to seek an illumination that is as uniform as possible over the whole area of the title. The simplest and best light is sunlight out of doors. Indoors near a french window, open or without curtains, is satisfactory if a mirror or a sheet of white card is used as a reflector to even up the light; or the board may be placed between two windows and illuminated by mirrors at either side. Sunlight gives the strongest contrast and the brightest colours; on a cloudy day the result is softer and colours have a colder cast.

With artificial light, two identical bulbs are used, one on each side of the title, at the same distance from it and forming an angle of about 45° with the lens axis. If only one lamp is available, it should shine as perpendicular as possible to the board. The greater the distance, the more even the illumination.

An electronic flashgun mounted directly on the camera usually gives too intense a light at such short range, and as it is above the lens, it does not even point at the centre of the title card. A flashgun should therefore be employed only if it can be fired away from the camera on a lead. With all types of lighting you will be wise to use a lens hood, and if the title is made on glossy paper or card, beware of reflections from the surface.

If you decide on a coloured background, choose a hue that is in harmony with the general tonality of the feature. Dark green is suitable for most plain titles. Pale blue is useful of it is desired

Double-mounting a title. The original slide includes a large area of sky.

to show texture or to throw shadows. Red is aggressive and nearly always looks wrong. It is worth noting that whereas in movies white lettering on a dark background is usual because of the unpleasant scintillating effect of a light screen, this does not apply with slides, and a black title can be very effective on a pale ground, particularly if it is superimposed on to a clear section of a transparency, such as a sky area. This is done not by double-*mounting*.

DOUBLE-MOUNTING OF TITLES

In order to work out the proportions of the lettering, the slide chosen to form the background is projected on to a piece of white paper and

Preparing the lettering on a white ground, in a position corresponding to the sky area in the original slide.

Slide of lettering and original transparency sandwiched together.

adjusted until it is the size that you wish to make the title (according to the distance from which it will be photographed). The transparency must not be too dense, but on the contrary have been fairly generously exposed, and the area selected for the title should be very transparent. The limits of the entire picture and those of the title-area are lightly sketched in pencil on the paper, and these outlines are then used as a guide to the size and placing of the lettering.

The black-on-white title is then photographed either directly on to colour reversal film, or if you have darkroom facilities it can be taken in monochrome and printed on positive film. The former method is obviously less bother though it may seem rather extrava-

The completed slide.

gant – but, after all, it's only one frame. If it breaks your heart to 'waste' colour on a black title you could always use coloured letters, but don't be surprised to find the result a bit gaudy if the picture-slide is already rainbow-hued. With reversal stock, exposure should be on the full side so that the white paper comes out as clear film. After development, the title shot and the background picture are simply sandwiched together in the glass mount. The film is so thin that focusing is no problem, but to be on the safe side place the lettering-slide first (emulsion against the glass) so that it is in the same plane as the other transparencies in the projector. An added refinement is to re-photograph the sandwich and so obtain a single slide. Copying can be useful in other ways too, such as the production of black-and-white negatives or the modification of the colours of a transparency, so it is worth devising a simple installation with which good copies can be made when needed.

COPYING

In order to reproduce a slide you must have a single-lens reflex with extension tubes or bellows enabling a 1 : 1 ratio (or more if you should wish to take just a part of the transparency). The camera must be firmly fixed to a stable support and carefully centered on the slide to be copied. In a horizontal layout, the transparency will be held upright in a small cardboard or wooden stand, with a piece of opal glass between it and the lamp behind in order to diffuse the light. Once the distances have been accurately worked out, the different elements can be attached permanently to a board. This simple method is quite good for occasional work, but as you will know if you have made prints by projection in a darkroom, the vertical system used for enlarging is much more practical.

A tripod could be used with the camera set to point straight down between two of its legs, but if you have an enlarger the set-up shown in the illustration is to be recommended. The camera is fixed in place of the enlarger head, and under it on the baseboard where normally stands the easel, is placed a light-box. This is a plywood cube measuring about 8 in. on each side. One side is left open, and in the top is cut a hole $1\frac{1}{2}$ in. square. The interior is painted white. If the slide to be copied is still in its original cardboard or plastic mount, it is simply laid over the hole (which of course could be larger if one wished to reproduce $2\frac{1}{4}$ in. (6 cm $\times$ 6 cm) transparencies). If the slide has already been placed in a glass mount, any dust spots should be carefully cleaned off with a soft brush. A small black cylinder or other form of mask should be placed around the slide to shield it from any stray light coming from above it. A piece of white paper or card is placed in the box at an angle of 45°, pointing towards the open side.

There are three possible sources of illumination: sunlight, electronic flash, or the beam of a slide projector.

The rays of the sun can fall directly on to the angled sheet of paper in the box, or be reflected on to it by a mirror. Daylight type film is used, of course, but remember that the colour of the light varies according to the time of day, and also that if the walls of the room in which you are working are brightly coloured this may affect the rendering. Through-the-lens metering is the ideal method of exposure calculation, but if this is not available, a meter can be placed against the slide and the reading multiplied by four in the case of a 1 : 1 ratio (by using slow shutter speeds; the lens should be kept stopped down as far as possible).

An electronic flashgun may be pointed at the paper from the side, or if preferred it can be placed in the bottom of the box (pointing

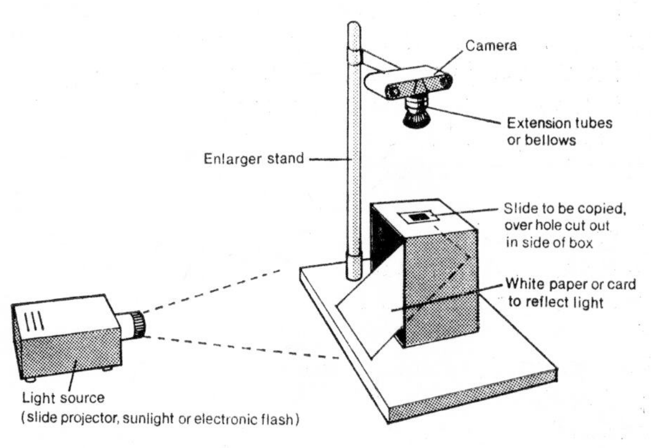

An enlarger stand used for slide copying.

up at the slide) under a piece of opal glass. In theory the colour is balanced for daylight, but with some guns it is a little cold. Gelatine filters type 81 or 81A may help, although even the palest are sometimes too strong and a certain amount of testing will be necessary to find the best combination. It may well be that a simple sheet of tissue paper, or the thin paper used by typists for making copies, will suffice. Although white in appearance it is in fact slightly yellow, and when placed over the glass, which in turn is placed over the flashgun, it gives just the needed warming effect.

With the flash pointing straight at the slide the light is very intense and the diaphragm may be as small as *f*11 or *f*16 with a film of 50 ASA. But if the flashgun is held outside the box and directed at the angled white card, more exposure will be needed, so a faster film can be used in order to keep the lens opening small.

The beam of a projector pointing at the sloping white card from about 2 or 3 ft away is the most practical source of illumination. The main advantages are that, unlike daylight, its intensity does not vary, and the exposure can be much longer than either sun or flash, giving the possibility of masking off a section of the image during a part of the time (the equivalent of 'dodging' or 'shading' when making prints by enlargement in the darkroom).

Artificial-light type film should give good results. Daylight film will require a conversion filter, 80B or 82B according to the whiteness of the projector bulb. If the filter is of the inexpensive gelatine variety, fix it in front of the projector lens to tint the source of the light rather than before the camera lens where it may cause slight unsharpness.

With this form of illumination, the copying should be done in the evening or in a darkened room, as any daylight falling on the card would alter the colour rendering and also affect the exposure.

In all three cases, the softer gradation of high-speed colour film makes it preferable because copying increases contrast. If the slide is to be reproduced in black-and-white, a fine grain film should be used and given full exposure with minimum development to obtain a fairly soft negative.

ALTERING THE SLIDE BY COPYING

Once you have found, by means of a series of tests, the best combination of lighting, exposure and perhaps filter to make a good copy of a slide, it will be a simple matter to modify the result. It is sometimes possible to improve a dense, underexposed slide by rephotographing it.

Washed-out, overexposed colours cannot be restored, but a pale transparency might blend more smoothly into a sequence if a darker version were made.

You may wish to add a touch of fantasy to a slide. A dream-like effect can be given to it by laying over the original slide a thin piece of clear glass lightly coated with petroleum jelly; the diffusion produces a halo around the highlights – partial if the jelly is only applied to the glass in patches. Greater diffusion and distortion can be brought to the copy by using patterned glass, of which many types exist. Combined with coloured lights or gelatines, a completely new and dramatic picture can be made from a very ordinary transparency.

Used in this way, copying can become a remarkable tool for creative experiment.

A Personal Approach to Colour

Of all the questions that have been put to me after a show, the most extraordinary was asked by the elderly aunt of a friend of mine, whom I had invited to see some holiday slides. 'The pictures are very pretty,' she said. 'Did you colour them yourself?'

After I had admitted rather shamefacedly that the colours were there by courtesy of the film manufacturer, it seemed to me that the lady viewed my work with considerably less admiration. This chilling occurrence took place some years ago, when black and white was still the basis of most photography and hand-coloured portraits were not unusual. Thinking back on the remark today, I find oddly enough that it contains a salutary lesson: it is a reminder that we rarely bring any *personal* contribution to the colour we are using, and indeed have lost the wonder of having colour at all.

COLOUR AND MOOD

Now that automation has taken over and many cameras have returned to the stage of 'you push the button and we do the rest', there is no excuse for not concentrating more on the actual image presented to the lens and trying to use the film in a more creative and imaginative way. Apart from the question of exposure, it has always been easier to obtain satisfying results in colour than in black and white. Perhaps because of this, many people who have attained considerable skill in modifying the results of monochrome reproduction by the use of lighting and filters do not seem to attach the same importance to employing colour consciously, as would an artist. Few amateur films or slides show any evidence of an attempt to express a mood or convey the feeling of a scene. Of course this is a difficult proposition for the producer of a travel or holiday record; but at other times it is possible to exercise a certain amount of control, if only by choosing the settings with an eye to the overall hue. And although filtering cannot be used in the same way as in monochrome, the weather and seasons play a big part in colour rendering. To wait for sunshine is quite unnecessary with today's emulsions, and remarkably attractive effects can be obtained in subdued light, in rain and in fog. In others words, if we cannot make the camera see *as* we want it to, we must try to make it see *what* we want it to.

Suppose you want to photograph a scene of young lovers that is cool, romantic and refreshing. Does that remind you of something? Of course: those advertisements, thanks to which the world has become aware that in order to obtain the maximum enjoyment from a menthol-fresh cigarette, it is wise to light it while standing by a mountain stream, preferably dressed in a green shirt. As it

The domes of St. Basil's in Moscow, painted in various bright colours.

Napoleon's signature (reproduced from a decree signed in 1812) in white on a dark background, appears symbolically over the previous image.

The same signature. It remains white, but the background is now bright red.

Moscow in flames. Red and black.

The army crossing the Berezina river. Orange, sepia and white.

The outskirts of Smolensk. Sepia and white.

The final stages of the retreat. Engraving in pale brown, grey and white.

Signatures (for the first time in his life, perhaps, showing signs of hesitation) black on very pale blue.

happens, the fine photography in that publicity gets over the message with great skill. This style, at its simplest, means eliminating contrasting colours. In a landscape with dominating cool hues, it is often suggested that you put a touch of warmth in the foreground or middle distance. On the contrary, try dressing the heroes in cold shades or white.

Similarly, on a grey, icy, foggy winter's day oozing melancholy, forget the spot of crimson. Make your characters wear grey or black. This is not, as it may sound, a waste of good colour film. The shot will still have hints of different hues, a sort of muted opalescence more attractive than many a rainbow-tinted scene. And it is only in colour that the winter feeling will really come across; for in monochrome, who could tell that the grass and weeds are frosty white?

Time of day is also a useful ally. Instead of correcting the warm glow of morning and evening light, make use of it – add to it, even, with a haze filter. Strong filters such as are made for black and white cannot normally be used, unless very eccentric effects are desired, but pale ones exist, in glass or the cheaper gelatine form.

In a slide-tape feature made for the bicentenary of the birth of Napoleon, I consciously tried to create a mood by the use of colour. Unfortunately I cannot show it to you in colour, but it is not difficult to follow in black and white. The stages of Napoleon's career are shown by means of paintings and engravings, and also various signatures (in order to demonstrate how they altered in keeping with the evolution of his character). These signatures are usually in black or a pale buff or parchment background, but I modified this in two cases. The overall tone of the Coronation (not reproduced here) is gold, so the appropriate signature is on this colour. In the 'Retreat from Moscow' sequence, the signature is white – at first on a dark background, so that by double-projection it covers the domes of the cathedral, as illustrated by picture No. 2, that shows the half-way stage between the first and second image.

The unfolding colour change takes place in eight slides that mix slowly from one to another (see pages 32–33).

The colour progression (or more precisely regression) is thus: normal bright hues swamped by red; the red slowly fading to white, the icy background of the final image washing all away.

In this case, colour control was simplified in that I was able to select the paintings to be reproduced and so chose only those that were in the required tonalities. With direct photographs, the task would naturally be more difficult. Paintings, coloured drawings and engravings make very attractive slides, revealing details that are unnoticed in normal viewing.

OUTDOOR 'STILL-LIFES'

A slide-tape feature consists of static pictures and there is no point in fighting that all the time. On the contrary, a series of 'still-lifes' can be very rewarding. There is one kind that could presumably also be called a landscape, but which depends for its success not on the appeal of fields and trees and mountains, but on a relationship between the elements that is immediately satisfying to the eye. The subject matter can be very humble: the weathered side of an old building, a rock, a tree stump, an expanse of grass. In itself the subject may be nothing, for the arrangement is everything.

As with controlled indoor still-life, composition is the result of selection and simplification. When you set up small elements, it is easy to refrain from adding those that are unnecessary. But with a large layout, such as a group of trees or houses, there are so many things that clamour for inclusion that it is difficult to avoid confusion. The photographer is often so preoccupied with a central object or a dominant feature that he fails to notice a cluttered background or another element that will turn out to be as noticeable in the finished picture as the main subject. Learning to see in this way is a laborious process for many people, but the results are worth the trouble of taking a few experimental shots.

STEREOSCOPIC PRESENTATION

There is no valid reason why a stereoscopic slide-tape feature should not be made, because this form of photography (better known nowadays as 3-D) still has its fans. The big boom began as early as the 1850s, when no home was complete without its stereo viewer, and the collection of pictures for sale in the shops grew into hundreds of thousands. The craze died out as quickly as it had come, only to reappear a hundred years later when Hollywood discovered Polaroid glasses. Still photography followed suit for a while, but the problems of viewing the two images, particularly by projection, have not been satisfactorily solved and remain too complicated for stereo photographs to become widely popular.

But it is worth noting that without resorting to true 3-D there are other methods of giving a feeling of depth to a picture.

WARM AND COLD COLOURS

It is well known that warm colours (red, orange, yellow) seem to come forward in space, whereas the cold greens and blues recede. The obvious example is a view of a distant landscape. A red flower taken in close-up against a cool background seems literally to stand out from the slide surface when it is looked at through the magnifying lens of a viewer; though less noticeable on projection, the effect is still very striking.

Atmospheric haze (used in conjunction with this colour regression), linear perspective, aerial perspective – and lighting – have long been used by painters; but there is one possibility that is typically photographic: it is known as selective focusing. As its name indicates, this consists of pinpointing the main subject and placing the background out of focus, not enough for it to be unrecognizable, but just sufficiently to detach it from the foreground.

SEPARATION OF PLANES

In stereo viewing, the three-dimensional representation often seems artificial because the scene appears to be separated into flat planes standing one before the other like so many cardboard cut-outs. But with one-eyed photography – especially when taken by certain types of camera where everything is sharp – there is on the contrary a tendency for all the planes to run together. To obtain a separation of the planes, the same factors apply as when one is seeking depth of field, that is to say the lens opening, its focal length, and the distance from which the photograph is taken; but they are, so to speak, used in reverse.

For example, a smaller stop increases the depth of field, but reduces the effect of separation until it disappears altogether; fairly wide lens openings are therefore necessary. The farther away the subject, the greater the depth of field around it; consquently it must be taken from as close as possible. A reflex camera is obviously the simplest for this purpose, preferably with the diaphragm used manually so that the degree of stopping-down can be controlled by eye. But people who like mathematics can no doubt calculate from a scale the amount of depth of field they will obtain. Here again the reverse of the usual technique applies, and the focusing should be as far forward as possible.

This method not only helps to give a feeling of depth to a flat picture, but is one of the principal ways of making the essential element stand out by attenuating the less important ones, which although necessary to the general rendering can sometimes be unduly aggressive. You must watch out for unwanted bright colours in the background (especially reds); their tendency to stand out becomes irritating when they are just out-of-focus.

Used with discernment, selective focusing can be a useful creative tool, and is certainly more than a mere technical trick.

COLOUR IS NOT ALWAYS PREDICTABLE

Unfortunately, no one, from the most experienced professional to the rankest beginner in photography, can predict exactly what will happen when he takes a colour slide. In black-and-white, the experienced user of a given film and developer combination can almost see his finished picture as he looks through the finder; but in colour it is another matter. There are too many variables to contend with.

The user is often to blame for the things that go wrong, but the manufacturer of the film and the processing lab are in some ways responsible for a certain amount of variability. A film emulsion is not a static material, but a continuing chemical reaction, and in colour film three emulsions are involved, hence three chemical reactions, plus interactions between adjoining emulsion layers. In spite of all this, the film is good for a relatively long period of time if correctly stored, and even when outdated may give pleasing results. The expiry date is usually based on storage conditions of 20–25°C, but could be extended for years if the film were kept in its sealed carton in a freezer. But colour balance would be seriously affected in a matter of hours if the seal were broken and the package put in a very hot place, such as the glove compartment of a car or even in a pocket on a hot day.

In designing a film, the manufacturer considers very seriously the way in which it will be used. Apart from the obvious factors of what kind of light will be employed – daylight, tungsten, flashbulb or electronic flash – there are also the questions of the range of shutter speeds, how rapidly the roll will be exposed, and how soon it will be processed afterwards. As most amateurs take their time in exposing a roll of film and getting it to the lab for processing, most companies build an extra tolerance into their product to compensate for these conditions.

To a great degree, the processing laboratory controls the colour balance of the finished transparency. It can vary not only from lab to lab, but within the same lab from day to day. Sometimes the film is consistently warm or consistently cool in colour rendering. This is not necessarily deliberate, but depends on dozens of external factors such as the condition of the water used, replenishment methods and working habits. These variations can even affect the emulsion speed.

EFFECT OF EQUIPMENT AND USER

Complicating the whole picture is the equipment used by the photographer to expose the material in question. His meter might be off (or he might use it improperly), his shutter might be slower than he thinks, so that a 1/125th would be closer to 1/90th of a sec, or his lens could have a warm or cold cast.

Many people who use colour film are not aware of the real colour of the original subject. They don't look at it analytically, but merely press the button and expect to see a picture that looks not like the subject but like other colour pictures that they have seen. To make this lack of attention even more confusing, the eye has an ability to compensate for differing light sources, but the film does not. An example of this is the photographer who is surprised that the pictures he took in the rain are blue. If he had been able to analyse the light when he exposed the film, he would have seen that the subject was, in fact, blue – although it is true that some emulsions do emphasize the effect.

The colour temperature of daylight ranges from 5000–25 000K. One film is supposed to handle all these situations, but it interprets each in its own way, producing a range of hues. Luckily, most of them are acceptable; and as we have seen, the variety of daylight is interesting to exploit. But when you are not trying to show the light that actually existed (for instance in very close shots or portraits) remember that colour reflects from walls, trees and other adjacent surfaces.

Whenever you doubt your equipment, and especially before undertaking any important pictures, run off a series of shots duplicating as closely as you can the conditions under which you expect to take them. By doing this, you are testing your whole system of photography to see if all the apparatus works well together. It doesn't really matter, after all, if your meter reads high and your shutter is slow so that the two cancel each other out; what does matter is that you should be able to use your equipment to produce consistently good – and, as far as possible, predictable – results.

Recording the Sound

When tape recorders first appeared on the domestic market, amateur film makers felt that their prayers had been answered. Here at last was the missing element that would make their work the equal of the professionals. Unfortunately, many of them soon discovered that it was not easy to obtain good sound, far less so than to get good pictures. In fact it is not a simple matter for the professional, although he may be surrounded by a studio full of magnificent equipment.

But the maker of a slide-tape feature has one big advantage over his colleague the amateur movie maker: he need not be obsessed by synchronization. It is usually necessary to project a film while recording its soundtrack, which not only can transform the work into a marathon race but bring problems such as the accidental picking up of projector noise. It is perfectly possible – and indeed preferable – to note down the timing of the slides and record the track separately, in peace and tranquillity of mind. And if something should go wrong, that part can be re-recorded at leisure.

In order to grasp the technical aspects of tape recording it is necessary to have an idea of its basic principles, so let us begin at the beginning.

FROM CYLINDER TO TAPE

Many people suppose that magnetic recording is a recent invention, but in fact it dates from the beginning of the century. It was in 1900 that a Danish engineer named Valdemar Poulsen patented a machine based on an idea that had been discussed in scientific magazines a few years previously. This aimed at replacing the mechanical principle of Edison's phonograph by a system utilizing electricity to capture the vibrations caused by sound waves. Edison had attached a cutting needle to the centre of a flexible disc known as a diaphragm, and allowed it to rest against a revolving cylinder covered with tin-foil. The spiral groove it traced appeared as a succession of humps and hollows. On playback, the motion of the needle in the grooves was communicated to the diaphragm, causing it to give off vibrations similar to those of the original sound. But the surface noise made by the needle scratching on the tin-foil, and later on the wax disc that replaced it, together with the short duration of the recording, made certain scientists seek for a radically different method. Poulsen was the first to succeed in applying the magnetic principle to a working machine.

His *telegraphone* made recordings on a steel wire which was unrolled at a constant speed between the poles of an electro-magnet. On playback the sound was listened to on headphones. The basic idea is the same today, the main difference in practical use being that the bobbin of steel wire is replaced by a reel of plastic ribbon a $\frac{1}{4}$ in. wide coated with particles of iron oxide. Headphones are still employed, but only when it is desired to monitor the recording; normally the sound is heard by means of a loudspeaker. The electro-magnet which is the heart of the system has been reduced from a large iron structure wrapped in coils to a tiny recording 'head'.

Sound waves are transformed by a microphone into variations in electrical current; these are transmitted to the recording head which in turn feeds them on to the tape. But the impulses are very weak and must first be amplified. This also applies in reverse: the feeble current of the reproducing head is amplified before passing to a loudspeaker which transforms it into vibrations in the air. On most tape recorders the same magnetic head serves for recording and playback, but certain professional machines have two separate heads. This enables the recording to be controlled a fraction of a second after it has been made.

The magnetic impulses applied to the iron particles of the tape behave in an ideal manner for our purpose: they are so stable that the tape can be played over and over hundreds and even thousands of times without any change in the quality of the sound, yet they can be wiped off instantly if desired, leaving the tape in its original state ready for a new recording to be made on it in place of the old one. The original recording is neutralized (erased) by means of a second electro-magnet (a third, in the case of the professional equipment just mentioned) charged with alternating current (a.c.). As the tape on a recorder always unwinds from left to right, the erase head is placed on the left of the recording head, so that the tape is neutralized before it arrives in position for a new recording. The erase head is automatically switched off when the tape is played back.

The characteristics of the electronic components of a recorder are very important, but the mechanical part of the equipment is just as vital to the quality of the sound reproduction. The motor must transport the tape at a rigorously constant rate across the recording head, at one of several different speeds which must be identical with those of other recorders. The slightest irregularity in the movement results in a flutter or 'wow' which is very noticeable, particularly in the case of music. Inaccurate speed produces a higher or lower pitch when the tape is played on another machine.

SOURCES OF SOUND

It is a mistake to think that all the sounds to be recorded must pass through a microphone. The purpose of the microphone is to trans-

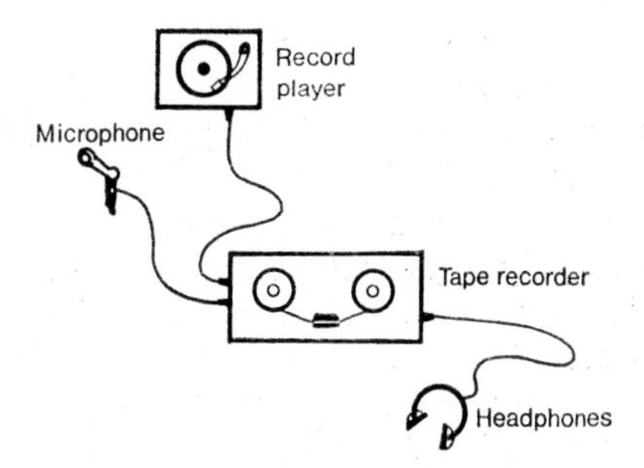

Making a soundtrack with a basic recording set-up. Most good recorders have at least two separate and mixable inputs. It is only necessary to plug the microphone and record player into them. Control of the volume of the input levels is simplified for a recordist if he wears headphones, plugged into the output of the tape recorder.

form into electrical impulses the vibrations made in the air by sounds. If this transformation has already taken place, there is no point in reversing the impulses back into sound in order to start all over again, which is what actually happens when we place a microphone in front of the loudspeaker of a record player or radio. To double the circuits in this way is quite unnecessary and in any case gives poor results, because the sounds picked up from the loudspeaker are not quite pure. They are more or less distorted

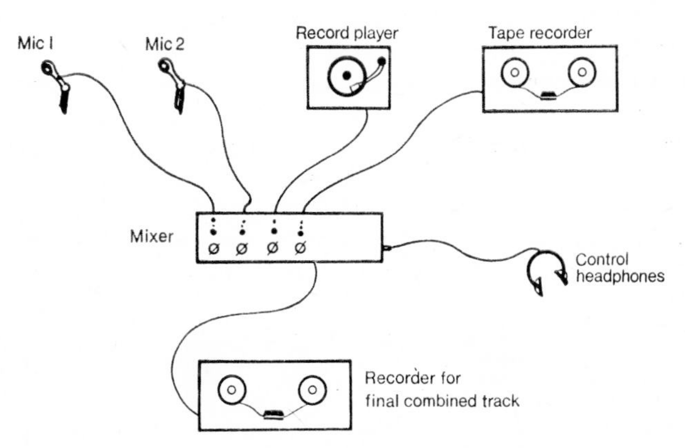

A more complex method of making a soundtrack, with a mixer linking together two microphones, a record player and a tape recorder. The output of each is controlled before being combined with that of the others and fed into the final recorder.

according to the quality of the amplifier and loudspeaker and by reverberation around the room and in the air before they reach the microphone. Moreover, the microphone picks up other noises, such as a ticking clock, traffic outdoors, running taps and so on.

The correct method is to take a low-level signal from the record player or radio directly to the recorder by a cable plugged into its input socket. (Many modern radios and record players are fitted with such an output.) For a simple soundtrack consisting of a commentary and some music from discs, the microphone is fed into one input and the record player into another (they are indicated on the recorder). For more complex tracks requiring, for example, two microphones, a record player and another tape recorder, a mixer should be used. This is a small unit containing several input sockets as well as volume controls and switches that enable the levels of the incoming sounds to be blended together correctly before being fed into the tape recorder.

ACOUSTICS

The reverberation or acoustics of a room play an important part in the reproduction of live music and speech. When a recording is made in the open, all sound comes directly to the microphone, because there are no reflecting surfaces nearby. In an enclosed area, one part of the sound comes directly and the other is reflected from the walls. As the reflected sound has travelled farther, there is a time-lapse between the two. Experiments have shown that this echoing effect makes speech more easily understandable, but the effect must be very slight. It is essential to the sharpness and clarity of music, which appears muffled and flat without it. In ideal conditions there should be only a single echo, that is from one wall, and the time-lapse should be short; in a large hall or church the pause between the departure of the original sound wave and its return is so long that speech becomes incomprehensible. But the long period of resonance adds power to the notes of an organ.

In recording studios, the walls and ceilings are covered with specially designed materials, some of which absorb the sound while others reflect it, in order to maintain a good balance. In the home, soft furnishings such as carpets and curtains have good sound-absorbent properties. An interesting experiment is to record the same text in different rooms. The living room and bedrooms will be found to provide the best acoustical qualities, whereas the kitchen is much more harsh and the bathroom an echo chamber. These last two are therefore not suitable for the normal recording of a commentary, but their hard sonority can be useful for special effects.

MAKING A TEST RECORDING

Before starting work on the actual recording, you will naturally make a test to ensure that everything is operating correctly and that the reproduction is good. The first thing to check is the level of the recording. If it is too high, the tape becomes over-modulated and the sound muffled and distorted. If it is too low, the volume has to be increased on playback, and background hiss is amplified. The recording must be as strong as possible without distortion, which is to say that the level indicator should be almost at the maximum end of the scale. Once you have found the right level, do not attempt to alter it during the recording unless there is a very great variation. The result must be as uniform as you can make it if you are to avoid having to adjust the controls during playback.

A continuous humming noise on the tape is not necessarily due to a recording fault but may be caused by a plug from the electrical lead or one of the connecting cables having been placed the wrong way round in its socket. If the plugs are of the two-pin variety, you need only remove them one by one, give them a half turn and replace them in their sockets. Once you have found the correct positions, you can put a tiny spot of paint on the socket and the plug so that in future they are always lined up the right way round. But with triple-pin plugs the connections will have to be remade. Another cause of hum could be that the microphone leads are too long or not sufficiently insulated.

The tone controls of recorders often operate only on playback, but if those on your machine affect the recording also, make sure that they are adjusted to the speech of the narrator. The treble is especially important for clarity, but too much 'top' can eliminate the deeper tones of the voice.

If music from a record or another tape is to be played at the same time as the commentary is being read, the levels of both should be noted. When the music alone is transcribed, it is maintained at full power, but when the narration starts, the input from the disc or the second tape must of course be lowered so that it does not swamp the voice of the reader. In order to control these different levels accurately, headphones are really necessary. They are plugged either into the recorder or into the mixer if one is being used. The 'stethoscope' variety is very light and convenient.

Should you decide to enlist the aid of a friend or two in making the recording, be sure that you have prepared your equipment and mastered its technicalities before they arrive, as nothing is more dampening to enthusiasm than to be obliged to wait while someone is fiddling with cables and plugs. Explain clearly what you aim to do, and hold a rehearsal. A microphone has a paralysing effect on many people, so keep the atmosphere calm and friendly. Some liquid refreshment will be welcome, particularly to the parched throat of the narrator.

COMMENTARY

The form of microphone provided with the home tape recorder is usually engineered to collect sound in an all-round manner, and, as has been said earlier, this can present a hazard because a large amount of unwanted sound is picked up in addition to the speech. Also, this type of unit often has a limited frequency response which gives a hard and tinny quality to the human voice. If you have such equipment, experiment with speaking at an even distance all around the microphone (about 3 or 4 ft away) and note on playing back the tape if the speech quality varies. The sharpest sound will probably come when the voice is directly in front of the microphone, tending to dull as it moves to the sides. In this case, as the speaker will be fairly close to the microphone, it is better to use its 'dull' side when reading the text. As a principle it can be said that the less directional (or 'wider') the microphone, the nearer it should be placed to the source of the sound.

A 'ribbon' microphone has a better frequency response and picks up the sound fore and aft, but not at the sides. With the speaker about two feet away, the quality of the reproduction is excellent. The only inconvenience of this type is that if it is used too close it is very sensitive to clicks and pops in the speech. The third kind of microphone is the dynamic or moving-coil type. This is a first-class unit, but is relatively expensive.

The microphone should be fixed to a heavy support or suspended, to avoid picking up vibrations from the floor. Beware of extraneous noises such as passing cars or motorcycles, or even low-flying aircraft! Not everyone can set up a soundproof cabin, which in any case often deadens the tone of voice; but cushions and thick curtains help a good deal. Some people like to read standing up, others sitting down. In either case the narrator must be careful to hold the written text in such a way that the rustling of the script is not recorded. It should of course be written or typed on one side of the paper only, to avoid having to turn it over. If you are of a very cautious nature, you can paste each sheet on to a thin piece of card.

RECORD PLAYER

Some amateurs and many clubs make use of two record players linked together to produce *mixing,* which is to say that one disc fades in over the top of another which is fading out. This is certainly handy to have when recording a motion-picture soundtrack, as it makes easy a change of rhythm or mood without interrupting the projection of the film. But such rapid juggling is not necessary with slide tracks, and one might as well invest the extra money in another recorder (or a stereo machine instead of a monaural one). The mixing can then be done by re-recording or multiplay. From the purely aesthetic point of view, it is more satisfying to end or begin the music at an appropriate point, rather than to allow one to 'clamber' over another. In any case, it is difficult to find the groove one wishes to play on an LP record, whereas the exact spot can easily be found if it has first been taped.

A certain routine must be adopted when taping a disc in order to avoid picking up the crackles and scratching noises that may be made when placing the stylus on the record:

1. Lower to zero the volume control of the tape recorder.
2. Press the recording control while retaining the mechanism by holding down the pause key.
3. Place the stylus of the record player on the disc, a groove or two before the required passage begins.
4. Release the pause key to set the recorder in motion.
5. Turn up the volume.

It is helpful to have a small lamp fixed low by the side of the player, lighting the record obliquely so as to accentuate the loud and soft passages of the grooves.

PLANNING THE TRACK

The timing of some slide-tape features is based on the length of the paragraphs in the commentary; other depend on the flow of the images; in most cases a track contains elements of both styles. Whatever method is adopted, it is essential to note down a plan on paper in advance, giving the approximate length of each passage. While you are editing the slides, you will already be thinking of the sound accompanying them. By the time the visuals are completed you will have a general conception of the whole. With this in mind, make a chart containing five columns:

1. The number of the slide.
2. A very brief description of it or a little sketch (you will not be able to remember each and every one in its order).
3. The number of seconds for which each slide is to be seen, as closely as you can tell from the silent projection. By reading the

text aloud while showing the slides you will be able to time the passages fairly accurately; the length of the music or effects will vary according to the content of the picture or the general rhythm of the production.

4. The text itself, double-spaced so as to leave plenty of room for eventual alterations.
5. Music and effects, with indications concerning the records or tapes to be used. If there are many changes of disc, a small adhesive label can be fixed to each, bearing a reference number for easy identification during the recording session. The number will also be noted in this column.

With such a chart, it is possible to record the track without projecting the slides at all.

SPECIMEN PROJECTION CHART

Slide No.	*Brief description*	*Screen time of slide in sec*	*Text*	*Music and effects*
Start				
1	"Presents" title	7	—	"Tintagel" (Arnold Bax) from start
2	Title: "A Cornish Legend"	10	—	Continued
3	Man against sky	11	Almost a year had gone by since the last time that Mark had stood here and looked down, and every detail of the scene gave him pleasure.	Fade down music
4	*ditto* Head and shoulders	12	It was good to be home, and he was suddenly aware of all the things it stood for, but also of how easily they might be lost. . . .	Continued
5	View from clifftop	10	—	Fade up music
6	Clifftop, Mark in foregd.	9	The sound of the sea was all about him, and the salt taste on his lips.	Music down, mix in waves and seagulls

Note: For presentation with a single projector, it is necessary to add *the length of time taken by the slide-changing* to the actual screen time.

If you possess just one record player and one monaural tape recorder, it is essential for you to have an assistant in order to record even such a straightforward track as this. However diverse may be your talents, it is too much to expect that you will be able to concentrate on starting up the machinery, changing the records and watching the recording levels while simultaneously trying to put some feeling into the reading of a text. But everything becomes more relaxed if you can use two recorders, or a stereo machine that can transcribe from one track to the other. With this equipment, commentary and music can be taped separately and blended together afterwards. An error in either does not mean that the entire recording has to be started all over again. This method is becoming increasingly popular.

USING TWO MONAURAL RECORDERS

It is up to you to decide whether you wish to tape the commentary or the music and effects track first. If the timing has been carefully worked out, the latter is perhaps preferable. You can take as long as you like, recording a snatch of music, stopping the tape, starting again. A mix can be made with the record player and the second recorder on which the required music has been taped. These original tracks should be recorded if possible at 7½ ips, not only to keep the quality required for re-recording, but to simplify any editing by cutting. Even a flaw of only a quarter of a second can easily be removed when it represents almost two inches of tape.

Once the music track is completed, the first tape recorder is plugged into the second via the 'radio' input. The narrator listens to the music track on headphones while reading the text into the microphone. If all is well, the recording can be made in one go; but if it is necessary to stop the tapes, use the pause key to avoid any 'clonks' that would have to be cut out afterwards. This method can be used with one stereo recorder, on condition that it has a system enabling one track to be played back while the other is recording.

If such a machine is available as well as a second recorder (this one not necessarily stereo) it becomes possible to tape the commentary quite separately, i.e. without the narrator hearing the music track. This presents distinct advantages. If the reader is not the author of the production, he or she need only come when required: the text can be spoken at leisure, without considering the background music; if a mistake is made, the tape can be stopped, wound back to the previous phrase and started again. When the track is satisfactorily completed, it can be used over and over during the mixing with music and effects.

But the snag here is to fit the text exactly into the right place, and especially to know when the volume of the music should be lowered (it has to be faint behind the words, but when there is a lengthy gap in the commentary it should be increased to normal volume). The lowering of the volume should be gradual and begin a second or two *before* the text starts up again. If the narrator has not taken the timing into account, how can one know on re-recording exactly when to adjust the controls? There is, fortunately, a simple solution.

POST-CONTROLLED TIMING

When the commentary is read 'live', in synchronization with the pictures and music, the narrator leaves an interval between the paragraphs of the text which varies according to the projection time of each slide. If there is a lot to be said, the paragraphs follow one another very rapidly; but if the phrases are short, the reader must wait until the next image is ready to appear. Several pictures in succession may have no spoken accompaniment at all, but only music or effects; the gap in the narration is then of many seconds or even minutes. In the method which could be described as 'post-controlled', the narrator takes no notice of the actual length of the intervals, but leaves only *a uniform interval of* 4 *sec* each time.

When you copy this tape with the other one of music and effects, you stop the text manually, a couple of seconds after each paragraph, by means of the pause key. When the next phrase is due to begin, you release the key, knowing that two seconds later the narration will begin again. You can therefore lower the volume of the music when required, just before starting up the text. When there is to be a gap in the narration, you stop its tape with the pause key and increase the musical background to normal level. If one of your recorders is stereo and the other mono, use the monaural one for the voice track, as you will be starting and stopping it all the time, whereas the music track, running in continuous synchronization with the final copy, will be one track of the stereo recorder.

It is of course possible to make visible marks on the tape itself with a felt pen (make sure it dries completely; some will not 'take' at all on tape) or by means of little adhesive patches. The mark is lined up with another made on the recorder itself. This is a handy system for the occasional editing job, but it must be admitted that with a long text it can become tedious.

SOUND EFFECTS

Here is a short, true anecdote which has a bearing on the subject of sound effects:

THE SOLITARY HUNTER

Night had fallen over the vast forest and the solitary hunter felt a sudden chill as small, mysterious sounds surrounded him on all sides. Sounds that resembled whispers, murmured confidences or threats. How true it is, he reflected, that Nature is never silent. He remembered having read somewhere that even in the most profound abysses of the ocean deeps, long imagined by poets as regions of utter stillness, strange noises had been recorded, leading some scientists to conclude that even the creatures who lived under the sea were not as mute as they were thought to be.

An agonizing cry tore the air apart. This hideous call – seemingly half animal half human – was echoed by another and yet a third, each closer to the hunter, who held his breath so as not to reveal his presence. But one of the beasts had flaired him, and he could hear its approach: branches rustling, twigs snapping. The shriek resounded again, the breath of the creature was almost on him. The hunter turned and ran, clawing his way through the undergrowth – and sank with relief into the seat of the car that he had left parked a few yards away on the main road.

This time the hunt was successful. For several evenings, the hunter had taken his portable tape recorder into Fontainebleau forest, which although only 40 miles from Paris still harbours wild boar and deer, in order to capture the calls of the stags during the mating season. I heard the recording at a Christmas party. We listened to it in the dark, and while those ugly cries resounded, we all felt uneasy yet excited as we realised that this timeless drama had been enacted only a short distance from where we sat. The climax lasted less than a minute; yet those moments, by their realism, packed more punch than the most artfully contrived fictional thriller.

The study of wild-life is constantly growing in popularity, and nowadays those who can afford to go to Africa on safari often take a camera instead of a gun. Many others find considerable satisfaction at less expense by investigating the countryside near their homes. Until recently, the amateur was restricted to the visual aspects of this fascinating chase, for the most complex of still or cine-cameras was small and portable compared with the bulk and weight of recorders. Today all that has changed, and it is in some ways simpler to obtain a sound record of birds and animals than to photograph them. Although few people would be prepared to risk the very real danger of an experience such as the stalking of stags by night, there is much pleasure to be found in simpler things, of which birdsong is the most obvious and delightful.

RECORDING THE SOUNDS OF NATURE

Nearly all animals produce a range of quite complicated and varied sounds, and recent research in this domain has shown that these constitute a veritable language. Even the cries of a fowl as reputedly stupid as a hen differ according to whether it is laying, alarmed, pleased, calling another hen or defending its chicks. It is said that a bull has eleven tonalities of roar which range from the rallying call to the threat. Most remarkable of all is the 'language' of the bees, expressed by a combination of vibrations of the antennae and a sort of ritual dance. In this manner a bee can give a series of indications to the hive concerning distances, orientation, and obstacles to be overcome on the way to the plants.

From the technical point of view, there are two main factors to be considered when recording wild life: the difficulty of isolating the sound desired from surrounding noises, and the distance possible between the microphone and the recorder. This latter problem is particularly awkward when the sound to be recorded is faint and so requires considerable amplification, as is often the case. If the microphone is too close to the mechanism it can pick up the whirr of even a quiet motor, and the proximity of the machine itself and its operator will scare away timid animals and birds. A better solution therefore is to use a long lead, place the microphone on a support as far as possible from the recorder, and control the actual taping with headphones.

Some birdsong consists of extremely high-pitched notes which may be beyond the range of certain types of recorder, and it is wise to use a reasonably fast speed on all machines in order to obtain the best quality possible – which means that the slow-running cassette recorder is not very suitable. The fast rate also makes eventual editing-out of unsuccessful passages or a montage of different sounds much easier.

Selection of the correct type of microphone is important. Here, unfortunately, money raises its ugly head, for the inexpensive crystal mike which comes with the average recorder will not do. Its tonal range is often restricted, yet on the other hand it is extremely sensitive to wind, so that when it is used out of doors the slightest breeze is transformed into a storm over the Niagara Falls. Also, it is not sufficiently directional. Comparing once again microphones with lenses, it could be said that a telephoto is necessary to isolate the elements of the scene.

In order to record from a considerable distance, even a very directional microphone may have too wide an angle, and it becomes necessary to adopt a concentrating system which pinpoints the noises coming from a particular spot. This is usually a parabolic reflector in whose centre the microphone is placed, pointing towards the bottom of the bowl. With this method is becomes possible to operate from a distance of ten or twenty yards, and the effect of the wind and other unwanted sounds is greatly reduced, even totally eliminated.

Of course not everyone is willing to carry around a miniature Jodrell Bank or to spend hours in damp forests stalking wild animals. But even in towns there are fortunately still a few birds left to be lured near the microphone with seeds or crumbs (not *too* near: about two feet away is usual) and attempting to immortalize the barks or miaows of the domestic pet can be a good exercise in technique which will come in handy on other occasions. Lucky is the sound man, who, unlike the photographer, can use his test reel over and over again!

COMMERCIAL RECORDINGS AND ARTIFICIAL EFFECTS

If you have no urge to record natural sounds yourself, remember that many commercial effects discs are now available. In some cases the band devoted to each sound is very short, so to lengthen it you can record it on tape, make a continuous loop and copy it off on to another recorder. Make sure your loop does not get caught up in the machine: the simplest system is to pass it around a spare reel held loosely at a suitable distance from the recorder. The reel can be slipped on to a large nail fixed in a block of wood.

Sound effects must be used in slide-tape with greater discretion than in motion-pictures (see page 98). But they are not forbidden, and as we are dealing with technical aspects in this chapter, here are a few notes concerning them.

It can be fun to make your own effects, and building up a library of them is an entertaining and useful way of experimenting with recording. A well-captured or created sound has a significance of its own which makes the effort worthwhile, and you will be surprised to discover how evocative of certain aspects of life a few related sounds can be. Here to get you started are a few well-tried methods that may come in handy some day; beginning with the three most celebrated:

Horses' hooves: Everybody knows that pounding the two halves of a coconut shell on a tray of gravel, or a tile, or against each other, cannot be improved on. Harness of the type used for restraining babies can be shaken to add a jingle, if desired. This is a realistic effect and amusing to do, but the need for it is diminishing.
Thunder: An oldie if ever there was one! Shake a thin sheet of metal hanging from a hook. As a matter of fact I have tried it and it is not all that easy to obtain a convincing recording; you will have to fiddle around with the position of the microphone a good deal before hitting on the best angle.
Fire: Sheets of Cellophane or tracing paper kneaded in the hands close to the microphone. Rustle them loudly for a roaring inferno, softly for a bonfire. The latter effect is enhanced if you get a friend to snap thin sticks at the same time.
Rain: Point the garden hose in the air and let the spray fall on concrete. Vary the pressure for the intensity of rain required. Alternatively, you can try scattering iron filings on a metal sheet.
Wind: Simulated by sucking in air close to the microphone with the forefinger against the parted lips.
Lapping water: Wave the fingers about in a bowl of water. A plastic bowl is preferable, as metal gives a ringing sound.
Creaking effects: You can use two pieces of resined wood screwed together and twisted about, but oddly enough the best effects are obtained with a balloon. You draw a finger across the surface with varying degrees of pressure and speeds. Creaking combined with lapping water produces the sound of a rowing boat.

Balloons have all sorts of uses. By letting the air escape quickly, quite an impressive explosion can be faked. The same thing in a more gentle manner has been used in safari epics to portray a hippo expelling air as it surfaces. If jungle noises tempt you, you could continue by making your hippo surface with a splash and plunge back into the water. For this you will need a whole bucketful of water and a suction plunger on a rod, of the type used for cleaning sinks. Pull the plunger out of the bucket and then push it back into the water again.
Rippling stream: Plug up the wash basin. Turn on the tape and let the water trickle off the back of your hand.
Screeching car brakes: Scratch a pane of glass with a metal rod.
Slammed car door: Drop a heavy book on the floor.
Hissing steam: Plunge a hot soldering-iron in water.
A ship's siren: This evocative sound is reproduced by blowing hard across the neck of a bottle. The tonality can be regulated by putting water in the bottle.

Excited natives jabbering: Well, you can have a lot of fun jabbering.

VARYING THE SPEED

The different speeds on a recorder can be used to modify sound effects, by the simple process of taping them at one speed and playing them at another. For instance the striking of a small bell (or even tapping a glass with a pencil) recorded at $7\frac{1}{2}$ sounds like an imposing church bell when played back at $3\frac{3}{4}$ ips. Household motors can be transformed into all sorts of machines by slowing them down or speeding them up. If you would like a tree being felled, crumple some paper at a speed of $7\frac{1}{2}$ ips and listen to it at the ultra-slow $1\frac{7}{8}$ ips. If you don't have this but can borrow a second recorder, make the recording in two stages. You can of course go on doing this several times, using the next speed down or up. This, after all, is how musique concrète began. With a little practice, you could even end up composing your own, by taking simple sounds such as a note on the piano, bottles being tapped, or the plucking of stringed instruments. With a small loop of tape, one single sound can be repeated and re-recorded as a rhythmic pattern.

EDITING THE TAPE

However carefully the soundtrack has been made, it is probable that it will need some editing to render it perfect. Editing tape is a very interesting operation which can be as simple as removing 'clonks' and other small mishaps or as complicated as an entire remodelling of the track. Basically it consists of cutting out the unwanted parts and sticking the tape together again with a piece of special adhesive ribbon. The resulting join is inaudible and very strong.

Before beginning to use the scissors, make sure that nothing else has been recorded on the tape, or you will be cutting into that track as well! In order to determine the position of the sound you wish to remove, listen to that section attentively and then play it again at the slowest speed. To make it even slower, you can turn the take-up reel by hand while pressing down on the pause key. Remember that the sound you are hearing is located at the playback head; in order to see the exact spot you may need to take off the cover which protects the advance mechanism.

The actual splice is made as follows:

1. Cut the tape at the selected place. (If the scissors are metal, make sure that they have not become magnetized.)
2. Hold the two ends to be joined one over the other with a slight overlap and cut them together *obliquely*. It is important that

the join should be made at an angle, as a splice made straight across may not be completely silent.

3. Place the two ends very precisely edge to edge.
4. Stick them together with a small piece (about ¾ in.) of special adhesive ribbon applied to the shiny side of the tape. Make sure that the adhesive ribbon is quite parallel to the sides of the tape, and press it well down so that there are no air bubbles or creases. Ordinary cellulose adhesive tape must not be used, as it is liable to become sticky at the edges, and so attract dust and possibly damage the recorder heads.

There are various models of inexpensive splicers on the market which make it even easier to join the tape, because they provide guides to the lining up and cutting.

When a commentary is to be taped by itself, that is to say without any background music or effects being played at the same time (these being perhaps added later by the method already described on page 47), there are two ways of rectifying any errors made by the narrator.

1. He can stop immediately, and when the tape has been wound back to the end of the previous sentence, read again the sentence which contained the mistake.
2. Without any interruption in the recording, he can pause for one second, and then read that sentence again. The original version of the sentence is cut out after the recording has been completed.

Of the two methods, the second is to be preferred, because not only will less time be spent on the actual recording, but from the point of view of the quality of the text, it is obviously better not to interrupt its flow and oblige the narrator to find again the identical pitch of his voice, and perhaps an emotion that he was putting into his reading.

Note that in both cases the interruption or cut is made between two sentences. It is possible to eliminate a single word, but this is a much more delicate operation, because the exact lapse of time between one word and the next (a fraction of a second) must be respected, otherwise there will be a jump in the rhythm of the delivery.

MAKING A COPY OF THE TAPE

Once the soundtrack is completely edited, it is wise to make a copy of it, not only in order to obtain a tape which is free of splices, but also as a precaution. By always using a duplicate, you have the satisfaction of knowing that if the track should be damaged or even accidentally erased during a performance, the original is unharmed and another copy, of a quality as excellent as the first one, can be taken from it.

Two recorders and a linking cable are required. One end of the cable is plugged into the output socket of the machine on which the original tape is being played, and the other end into the input of the one used to make the new recording. The two recorders can be running at a faster speed than the original track, on condition that their speeds are identical to each other. This makes for quicker copying.

To start up the machines, the same routine should be followed as for taping a disc (see page 45), the only difference being that the

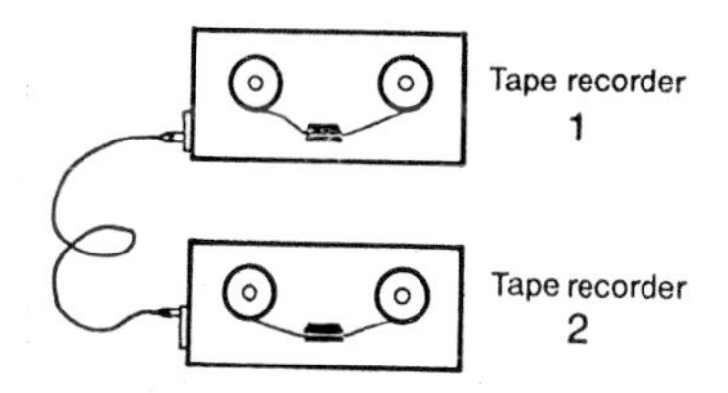

Copying a tape: A cable links the output socket of the recorder playing the the original tape to the input of the recorder making the copy. When taping a disc, the same procedure is used, except that a record player replaces the first tape recorder.

recorder reproducing the original soundtrack replaces the record player. Keep an eye on the modulation controls during the copying, and avoid over-saturation which causes distortion.

POSSIBLE DEFECTS

Here are a few of the more common faults that may be noted on a recording, and their possible causes:

Another track is heard at the same time A previous recording on the tape is not completely erased, either because it was extremely over-modulated or because the erase head of the recorder is worn or clogged with dust particles. Before making a recording on a tape that has already been used, it is wise to run it through the erase head (with the controls in 'record' position but without plugging in the microphone), and not rely on its being erased during the new recording.

Another reason for hearing two tracks at once could simply be that a tape containing two separate recordings made on a four-track recorder is being played on a dual-track machine.

Wow and flutter — The tape is running at uneven speed. There are several possibilities: bent reels catching the tape; slipping of the drive belts; insufficient tightness of the pressure pad; take-up axis warped; insufficient motor power.

Strong humming sound — Plugs making poor contact or reversed; microphone cable too long or not correctly insulated; microphone too near the recorder (so picking up the noise of its motor); or an electrical fault in the amplifier.

High-pitched whistle — Feedback (also known as Larsen effect) occurs when the microphone is placed too near a loudspeaker which remains operational during the recording. Part of the latter's output is fed back into the microphone, amplified and returned to the speaker, and so on in a continuous cycle. If you should use your recorder as a public address system, set up the microphone well away from the loudspeaker; and when recording, make sure the speaker is switched off, if this does not take place automatically.

Very weak and muffled sound — If the equipment is working normally, the reason for this is probably that the tape was inserted the wrong way round. The matte side must face the heads.

Good sound but weak, with a background hiss — The recording level was too low. It should be kept as high as possible without reaching oversaturation.

Narrator's voice sounds 'hollow' — The room in which the recording was made has too much echo. Choose a room with soft furnishings that absorb the sound, or hang heavy curtains near the microphone.

The soundtrack is pitched a little too high or too low — The recorder was not playing quite fast enough when the track was taped (pitch now too high) or is playing too slowly at present (pitch too low), due to its still being cold. It should be warmed up by letting it run for several minutes before use.

Short breaks in the sound — Could be due to dust on the heads, but a more likely reason is that the tape is too thick or too stiff, and occasionally loses contact with the head. This is particularly noticeable with four-track recorders, for which very thin and supple long-playing tape is recommended.

With a little practice, everybody can make a tape recording of excellent quality. But although it is relatively simple to operate, a recorder is in fact a complex and delicate piece of equipment. Handle it with care and keep it free of dust. Unless you have considerable technical knowledge, do not try to repair any faults in its mechanism yourself; consult an expert.

Preparing the Slide Show

Try this little exercise: think of the best photograph you have ever seen, in a magazine or on the walls of an exhibition. Compare it mentally with that depressing holiday snapshot somebody showed you last week. What made the difference? Both were taken with a camera, developed, fixed and printed on a piece of paper. Now think of the film you have most enjoyed, and compare it with . . . I was going to say 'some home movies' but there are plenty of boring professional films. What made the difference? They were all taken with a cine camera and projected on a screen.

The answer is that any successful presentation needs three elements: good basic technique, a dash of originality, and an elusive ingredient known as 'appeal'. Slide-tape, which is half-way between photography and cinema, needs them as much as if not more than either, for the basic simplicity of its technique (compared with film making) is apt to induce carelessness. The best incentive to good work is the thought that it is going to be shown in public, and the only way to improve is to compare the production with others. But entering a competition is an ultimate goal and we have not reached this summit yet! For the time being, let us consider the principles of this method of presentation.

First, then, we have a series of slides arranged in a certain order (in cinema, one would say 'edited'), and second, a magnetic tape recording which is played while the slides are being projected. Simple enough – but the main point to be grasped right from the start is that the tape should not be considered a mere accompaniment to the transparencies, such as a flow of 'background music' to travel pictures, but as an integral part of the presentation: image and sound must be planned together, as a whole, each complementing the other. Everybody loves a good story, and we should think of ourselves as story-tellers, even though the subject may not necessarily be a fictional tale. As in a film there should be a progression, each image carrying us a step forward.

The physical effort in editing transparencies is so much less than in putting a film together that there is really no excuse for not attempting it, and fortunately most people do. But oddly enough it is the order in which the slides were taken that seems to worry them most, although this cannot possibly matter to anyone but themselves, and is downright irritating when it leads to arguments between husband and wife as to whether the sunset over the Mediterranean was photographed before or after the visit to Capri, or whether the market in Seville is on a Saturday because if so the shot of oranges on a stall must have been taken before the spire of the cathedral which they visited on the Sunday. All that matters is the result *on the screen,* so if the Seville oranges look good coming after a grove of fruit-trees let's show them that way, even if they were taken three hundred miles and two days apart. But obviously if they are part of a sequence showing your daughter leaving the hotel, crossing the town to the market, buying the oranges and coming back again with them in her hand, it is in that order that they must be shown.

Just common sense? Naturally, for common sense is the basis of editing, although it is pleasant to spice it with fantasy once in a while. As a painter stands back from his canvas to see how he is progressing, so must we occasionally look dispassionately at our work and wonder how it can be improved.

You must decide as soon as possible the form the slide feature is going to take, or at least get a general feeling of its rhythm, for only then will you know whether you are going to need many transparencies or only a few, and whether some new ones will have to be taken to fill in continuity gaps.

TIMING AND TEMPO

Rhythm is important, and here again we can borrow from the film-maker's technique, the length of time each picture remains on the screen depending on the content of the slide: a distant shot with more to 'take-in' requiring longer than a closer view. The type of presentation affects the speed also, of course. A romantic evocation might tempt us to leave each slide for 15 – 20 sec, a tempo which would be rather languid for a brisk reportage, where 10 sec could suffice. The mechanics of slide projection necessitate a certain length of time, however, and brief shots of 3 or 4 sec duration which are current in cine-films, are out of the question. A screen time of 7 sec per slide can be considered a minimum. For a picture to stay longer than 20 sec, it must be either exceptionally good, or require some explanation – unless the text is at that moment particularly important and the author has decided to attract attention to it by lessening the visual impact.

How long should the *total* presentation last? If we average 12 sec a slide, 50 slides will last 10 min, and 50 well-chosen pictures represent quite an achievement. How pleasant when the lights go on to hear people say: 'What a pity, it's over already! Have you got another one to show us?' Far better to make three 10-min features than one half-hour opus.

A LINKING THEME

It is the fact of having a theme that distinguishes a slide-tape feature from a run-of-the-mill presentation of colour transparencies. So if we presume that you have already taken a number of slides and wish to make something a little creative out of them, the first thing is to find out whether a sufficient quantity can be grouped together to form a single, coherent subject.

Looking at them in a viewer is not the way to do this; it is better to project them fairly rapidly. Quite soon a general 'feeling' will emerge. Needless to say, for this first attempt you are not going to try to put together a complicated or even a very original presentation. A theme can be any number of different things other than the person or family in various situations as seen in most travelogues: it can be a poetic record, such as the passage of time from morning to evening; it can be light-hearted, as in a short French production called *Deux* that was little more than a list of items that go by pairs; and it can of course be a musical theme, in which case the visuals are chosen to illustrate the general mood evoked.

MAKING A SELECTION

First, you must ruthlessly eliminate the slides that are technically bad, showing gross over- or under-exposure or camera shake. (This sort of editing can be done more easily with pictures that are already

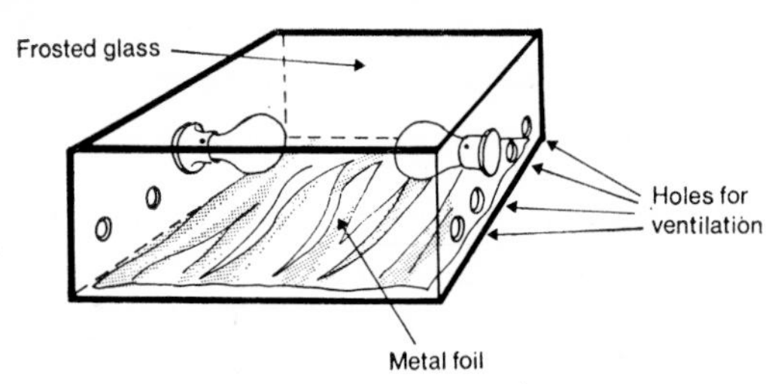

A light-box. The top consists of frosted glass, the bottom is lined with metal foil. Lighting can be by tubes or lamps (the latter need more ventilation).

a few months old. By that time, a certain detachment has set in which is more difficult to adopt when the transparencies have just returned from processing.) Those that are only slightly too dark, too light or blurred can be kept for the time being if they are otherwise interesting. When two or three pictures have been taken of the same subject, keep only the best one. Eliminate also those shots that are of a very personal nature; they can always be shown separately in a series intended for the family. Run the 'survivors' through the projector again. You will no doubt find that one particular slide would be better if placed before, or after, another. One image will strike you as the obvious one on which to end the series. Already some sort of form is taking shape. Beware of the slide that is *too good*! You may feel that it is in some way out of keeping with the rest, but is so beautiful in itself that you cannot bring yourself to remove it. I am afraid it will have to go, all the same. Console yourself by thinking that it might come in handy for some other series. It can be the first contribution to your library of 'shots for future productions'.

Earlier on I mentioned that the only way to judge slides was by projection. But once the selection is made, it is useful to be able to view them in groups, so that those that have affinities can be placed together. The best way to do this is on a light-box, which should be large enough to hold at least 40 slides at a time.

The light-box should be about 8 in. deep and be painted white inside. The top consists of a piece of ground glass, or even ordinary glass covered with a sheet of Kodatrace, and the illumination can consist either of two small bulbs, or preferably neon tubes as they do not get hot. Such a light-box can be bought commercially, but is very simple to make.

EXAMPLES OF SUCCESSFUL FEATURES

From a holiday trip to Holland in the Spring, one photographer brought back a series of slides that were of excellent colour and composition, but that seemed destined to make nothing more than a banal travelogue. On projecting them a few times, he noticed that many of these shots of windmills, canals and Dutchwomen in clogs had one thing in common: flowers, and in particular tulips, of course. He selected these slides and added to them a few big close-ups of tulips taken at a different time in his own garden. He then put together a commentary which spoke poetically of flowers and only incidentally of Holland. The result was a very beautiful production that was voted the best in his club's annual competition.

Another show was inspired by a little boy telling his parents that he had just learned at school that not only the human body but the whole world was mainly composed of water. This gave his father an idea for a fantasy in which his son would be so impressed by this thought that he would see everyone and everything transformed. He gathered together some shots of the boy and all the slides he had on the theme of water, then took a few extra shots, notably of a classroom where all the children were replaced by earthenware jugs. With a light-hearted commentary and entitled *Aquarium*, this amusing slide-tape feature won the major award in a leading French contest.

Two French friends of mine who had spent a few days in London brought back with them several hundred slides. They had all been taken in a hurry, and on the whole their technical quality was not too good. My friends asked me to help them to make something out of these pictures – no small task, as just projecting them took over an hour each time. It became clear that these visitors had taken a few public monuments because it was the thing to do, but that their main interest centred on people in the streets, and in particular those wearing unusual Carnaby Street clothes and mini-skirts, which at that time had just started to make an appearance. We decided that this would be the theme, and I chose about 80 shots of people and arranged them in sequences according to their type of clothes, in some cases contrasting the new style with the traditional British 'bowler and umbrella' look. The slides were projected very quickly, in time to a 'pop' tune. As *A Frenchman looks at London,* I showed this slide-tape feature at the 1969 Olympia Photo-Fair, where it went over very well.

HOW NOT TO DO IT

For my sins, I have sat through many hours of projections, and one of the most boring soirées was provided by a gentleman of means who had just returned from safari in Africa with a vast collection of colour transparencies. He presented them accompanied by a recorded tape which (no doubt to prove that no expense had been spared for our entertainment) was stereophonic. The quality of the recording was very good, as was the photography. The subject, although becoming rather hackneyed these days, was interesting enough. So what went wrong?

A certain amount of editing had been done, but mainly of a chronological order ('we left this place on Tuesday, and arrived here the next day'). This type of arrangement may be of importance in a business report, but is meaningless to anyone who has not participated in the event. Editing should always be a linking of the images and sounds as they *are,* not according to some exterior happening during the taking.

The sound was a mere accompaniment: technically, the 'stereo' consisted of a voice coming from a loud speaker on one side of the screen and monaural music from the other side. Thanks to this system the music was not even lowered during the narration; it was a long-playing disc of classical music recorded in its entirety, even the gap between the movements.

Instead of telling us interesting things we could not know about, such as his personal reactions to the adventure, the narrator spent his time describing the pictures on the screen.

As we were spared nothing, from the arrival in Africa to all the details of the preparation for the safari, the whole presentation was far too long.

All these remarks could apply to a motion-picture, but there was a strange thing inherent to the slides. Because their presentation was so similar to many travelogues, one expected movement but there was none. So that all those lions, zebras and elephants in their frozen attitudes looked stuffed! Instead of going so far to photograph them, a trip to a natural history museum would have sufficed.

So, you may well say, what was our traveller supposed to do with all his beautiful pictures? He had gone on a marvellous trip and was reliving it all. Yes – but the trouble with that argument is that the show was put on not at the Travellers' Club or the Explorers' Society but at a photo club. From that point of view it failed completely. Although there was a good basic technique, a total lack of originality soon turned into boredom a presentation which could have had a great appeal.

MOUNTING THE SLIDES

There have always been arguments for and against the principle of removing transparencies from their original mounts and placing them in special glass holders, and now that some manufacturers return the slides in attractive plastic mounts this may seem a waste of time and money. There are indeed many disadvantages to glass mounts: their expense, weight and bulk, the fiddly work of putting the slides in them and the difficulty in preventing specks of dust from being enclosed at the same time; with standard glass the risk of Newton rings; and, worst of all, the fear of damp or fungus eventually damaging the emulsion. I am not at all convinced that glass-mounting of transparencies can 'protect' them, rather the reverse, whereas with careful handling by the normal mounts, scratches and fingerprints are unlikely, and if the slides are kept and projected in magazines that is surely quite adequate protection. Consequently I never mount in glass the personal pictures kept for home projection.

However, for a public performance the problem is quite different: all the above disadvantages put together do not counterbalance the need for accurate focusing. In these circumstances, a 'popping' slide is intolerable. With dual projection, in particular, it is essential that each picture should be sharp as it appears on the screen. And as the chore of mounting must be done, one might as well make use of the possibility it offers for sandwiching and masking (see page 138).

There are various types of glass mount on the market. Some are slightly thicker than others, so it is wise to use the same make throughout a feature in order to avoid a change of focus. Needless to say the glasses must be absolutely clean before the piece of film is inserted. The simplest method is the best: a fine handkerchief and a little huffing and puffing. Better not use alcohol. You should always wait at least two or three weeks before mounting transparencies under glass; soon after development they are 'green' and humidity will be trapped inside the mount.

MARKING AND STORING

Each slide should bear an identification mark – the initials of the title, for instance – and the number of its position in the sequence. During the preparation, the slide will be in its original mount, so the identification number can be roughly marked in pencil for easy erasure if the order is changed after experimentation. When the final mounting has taken place, the identification and sequence number must on the contrary be applied in a permanent manner that will not smear and be clearly visible in a dim light. Anything written directly on plastic mounts, especially with a fine-pointed felt pen, will soon rub off, and a neater solution is to apply a small self-adhesive label in the corner. This is rather a fiddling job as the label must be carefully applied and well pressed down all around so as not to come unstuck, but the result is worth the trouble and it need not take too long if the identification mark and number are written on the labels in order *before* these are removed from their support for application to the mounts.

The marking should be the right way up when the slide is in position for projection – that is to say that when the picture is upside down the label is at the top of the mount. It will be placed in the left corner, as the right one is reserved for a red spot. I personally find that the identification number is sufficient, but most clubs and competitions still insist on this spot as a guide for the projectionist, so you might as well do things correctly. It can be applied with a touch of a large indelible felt marker.

To recap, let me repeat that the red spot is to be in the top right corner when the slide is placed in the projector; consequently, when the picture is viewed the right way up (and the right way round, so that any lettering is seen correctly) on a light-box, it will be at the bottom left.

The slides can either be kept in one of the many types of storage box that are to be found on the commercial market or, if automatic projection is used, left permanently in the magazines made to fit the projector. The latter system is less trouble, but magazines may take up more room than boxes, in which the slides are packed more closely together, and are more expensive. When dual-projection is used, it is practical to keep each production in two magazines or boxes, one with the odd-numbered transparencies, the other with the even.

Presenting the Show

However carefully you may have prepared your slide-tape feature, it will lose some of its effect if it is poorly presented. You may feel that it is rather absurd to speak of 'showmanship' when your audience consists of only a few members of your family and one or two friends, but it is not because you know them personally that they are not entitled to a comfortable evening. If you have to spend long minutes fiddling around with wires, turning chairs and finding a prop for the projector, your guests will be peevish before you start and you yourself will be likely to fumble and possibly put on a bad show. At its best, showmanship merely means knowing what is needed for good presentation and making sure that everything that can be prepared ahead of time has been done before the audience arrives. This chapter deals with the basic requirements for a satisfactory show at home, or eventually away from home – the same 'rules' apply then, only more so. Many of them are only the application of common sense.

In practical terms, you need a solid support for the projector and tape recorder, an arrangement of switches and leads that permits the use of the equipment and a room light without any acrobatics or hazard to the audience; if you have a coal fire, an effective fire-screen to prevent light falling on the surface of the projection screen; adequate seating; a screen of adequate dimensions set square to the projector, and a loudspeaker placed near to it.

Once the lights are out, the audience is at your mercy. Above all, be sure you keep them entertained, and if in doubt about including a particular series of slides, then *exclude* it: if wanted, the demand for an encore will give you the chance to show it. Make the setting-up, if it has to be done with the audience in the room, apparently effortless. Force people to sit in the best positions and to go upstairs to fetch their glasses rather than tell you afterwards that they were sorry they could not see. Plan any refreshment interval precisely, beforehand. Avoid switching on the projector lamp without a slide being engaged and flooding the screen with white light. This is a far greater annoyance to the audience which is staring ahead in all innocence than is sometimes realized by the operator whose eye is on his machine.

A FIRM SUPPORT

This is vitally important. The main attraction of slides is their superb quality compared with even the best movies; but for this to be appreciated the projected image must be absolutely static on the screen. With a flimsy support, a slight trembling sets in at each slide-change, especially if it is manually controlled; this trembling is considerably magnified on the screen. A sturdy table can be suitable especially if it is large enough to hold both the projector and the recorder; but the projector may be too low. Tilting may be inadequate or on the other hand may produce distortion known as 'keystoning'; it is better to raise the whole machine on a solid box or special wood block. Some users prefer an independent tilting device, made from two hinged boards with a long screw and nut at the front.

In theory, of course, the picture should be projected over the heads of the audience from behind the last row of chairs, in order to avoid having to leave a central gap. If people have to sit behind the projector, stray light may get in their eyes, and they can also be disturbed by the movements of the operator. But with the wide-angle lenses fitted on most slide projectors, this requires a rather large screen. Never wave the projector about while trying to balance it on odd books and keep switching it on and off; this is very bad for the lamp. Folding projection stands are commercially available that have the advantage of being easily portable, of taking up little room, and of having an adjustable tilt; for slide-tape, the type with a lower platform on which the recorder can be placed is practical. However certain makes are a little wobbly if the equipment they carry is lightweight – a defect that can also be noticed in the stands made by some enthusiasts from old kitchen trolleys, with shelves to hold the recorder as well as the slide boxes.

PROJECTION SCREEN

There are three problems here: the surface of the screen, its size and its shape. As I have mentioned before, the quality of a good slide is such that one might as well project it as big as possible. Certain types of screen are therefore unsuitable in view of their high cost in large sizes.

BEADED SCREEN

These give the brightest picture, but only to the persons sitting directly in front. At the sides the reflective power is very poor and can be even less than a white-painted wall. Beaded screens are usually recommended for long narrow rooms, but as few lounges are so designed they are rarely worth the extra money. If one sits too near them, the effect can be spotty. They are also fragile, become easily cracked if kept rolled up, turn yellow in daylight and are impossible to clean. It really is better to save the cash that a beaded screen would cost and use it to pay a little extra for a more powerful projector, which would have the advantage of being able to project in larger halls when necessary.

SILVER SCREEN

The good old 'silver screen' of the days of silent epics is just about obsolete. It is less bright than a beaded surface and has only a slightly wider viewing angle; from the extreme sides it is even worse. Aluminized screens came to the fore again a few years ago during the brief resurgence of interest in 3-D, because matt white or beaded screens are unsuitable for stereo projection (of the type wherein the viewer wears Polaroid glasses) as they 'depolarize' the light. Today, certain laminated metallic screens are available that are luminous and have a reasonably wide angle of view, but they are expensive and delicate to handle.

MATT WHITE SCREEN

These may not be as highly reflective as the other two types, but they are the least directional; there is hardly any light loss at the sides. They are also economical and available in large sizes. You have probably guessed by now that this is the kind of screen that I would recommend for slide-tape shows. A slide projector provides a brighter image than an amateur cine-projector; dare I say that until you have decided to invest in a screen you would probably project quite well on a white-painted board or wall. When the time comes for you to present your programmes in bigger halls, then the matt white screen will still be the best, for it is the most practical to install, the least prone to damage, can be cleaned, and gives a very good picture indeed on condition that you can offer it a sufficient light output.

SCREEN SHAPE

The shape of the screen depends on you. If you are using 126 cartridges, Rapid film or 6 × 6 cm, then you will naturally need a square screen, as you will if you shoot 35mm both vertically and horizontally. However if, as I hope, you eventually adopt the method of presentation by means of twin projectors that we shall be discussing later in this book, you will probably prefer to use 35mm in the horizontal format only in order to avoid the somewhat unaesthetic effect produced by the crossing of images; in this case a rectangular screen will be correct. A square screen becomes very unwieldly in large sizes, and the current trend to big and wide screens, added to their being easier to set up in an auditorium, may make you favour the rectangle.

AIDS TO PRESENTATION

A perfect blackout is greatly to be desired; you could perhaps obtain a sheet of hardboard that fits the window-frame exactly. Your screen might even be attached to (or painted on) the centre of this and the surround painted matt black, which will make the picture appear sharper and brighter. Some gadget-minded cinema-lovers fix a small motor to their curtain cords and open and close them over the screen by remote control, but this sort of thing seems rather passé nowadays, and it is unlikely that enthusiasts are still building gilded prosceniums in their home complete with miniature organs and coloured lights, as was being done not too long ago throughout Britain because, as one fanatic explained, 'just as an oil painting needs to be set off by a gilt frame, so also the screen needs an elegant surround'. Today, it is better appreciated that the necessary aids to polished presentation are a sharp, well-illuminated image correctly centered, and good sound reproduction. However a small *dimmer* for the room lights is a very acceptable gadget and the wiring up is no more difficult than for an ordinary light switch. Add up the wattage of the lamps you wish to dim and get a dimmer to correspond.

LOUDSPEAKER

The sound should of course come from the direction of the screen. At its simplest this means that the tape recorder is placed near it and started by a member of the audience, or even by the projectionist himself if he has allowed a few seconds of blank on the tape to give him time to leap to the back of the room before the track begins. But this is really a very crude method, and it is obviously preferable to make use of an extension speaker. With the recorder by his side, the projectionist can control the volume and tonality during the show; however well the track has been recorded, there may well be a need for slight adjustment from time to time.

Most people place the loudspeaker directly under the screen, but this is not the ideal position, as the spectators in the front row receive a full blast, but mask the sound from those behind them. If possible the speaker should be placed fairly high up and pointing to the back of the room (the opposite corner, if it is to one side of the screen).

SYNCHRONIZATION

As we have seen, a synchronizing unit is a very handy piece of equipment, but it is not absolutely essential to the slide-tape maker who is projecting his own productions. After a little rehearsing, it is quite easy to change the slides at a given moment, particularly if the commentary consists of short separate paragraphs. If you decide to do without a synchronizer at first, for Heaven's sake make this effort of memory and on no account record clicks or buzzes or bells on the tape to indicate the next picture, as is still done at some lantern lectures or on commercial postal conferences. This completely ruins any atmosphere you may be trying to create. If you have a stereo recorder, indications can be given on the second track to be heard only on headphones, the main track being played monaurally over the speaker; or the visible cue by means of a little bulb previously described can be mounted discreetly by the projector. A chart or booklet listing the shots and commentary together with the timing should always be prepared as a reminder; if you have not shown a particular production for a few months you will be glad to look through it before, and even during, the presentation. If the booklet is carefully prepared and if the slide-tape feature is a straightforward one (without too many long stretches of music or effects replacing commentary) it is quite possible to project someone else's production for him, just by following the indications.

CHECKS AND SAFETY MEASURES

Presentation, above all, means avoiding breakdowns and disappointments. Make sure you have at least one spare lamp, as nothing is more infuriating than to have the bulb blow out just as everyone is ready – but at a time when all the shops are closed. Give the slides a 'once over' before the show to check that they are all in sequence and the correct way up. See that the recorder is on the right speed for the tape. Like all things that are done smoothly and well, good showmanship generally passes unnoticed; but the audience is only too aware of bad presentation. In the home, there are only a few points to think of. Outside the home, matters are a little more complicated, but the effort is worth while.

OUTSIDE SHOWS

The man who has never carted his projector and recorder to a hospital, boys' club or church hall has not lived. The land should always be looked over first, the length of the throw checked, and audience size in excess of audio or projector capacity sternly refused.

If the meeting is to be held during the afternoon, find out if the hall can be blacked out. It's amazing how many organizers overlook this necessity, especially when they do not often put on film or slide shows. Slides have a slight advantage over cine-films in that they can be projected with a certain amount of room lighting, but it hardly shows them to their best advantage. If only part of the room can be correctly darkened, place the screen there. Fortunately most shows take place during the winter and in the evening, so there is no difficulty in darkening the room – except when treacherous lights from the street or from other buildings flood in by the uncurtained windows.

Find out where the room lights are switched off and on. If some lamps have to be left on over the exits, make sure they don't light up the screen; they can perhaps be shaded. And watch out for doors that may open during the show. Ask for them to be kept shut during the performance; if this is not possible, see that no bright light comes through from outside each time.

Apart from your usual equipment you will need the following items:

Extension leads for the current.
Extension cable to the loudspeaker.
Electric torch.
Spare plugs and adapters, screwdriver, cellulose tape, scissors.
Spare projector lamp.
A microphone that plugs into the recorder, to be used if needed as a public-address system.
Spare tape recorder, if possible.

In clubs, rope in two or three members as assistants, not only to help in the setting up (a large screen can be a problem if you are alone) but during the show, to keep an eye on trailing flex and the projector stand.

SELECTING THE PROGRAMME

Although the choice of a programme is a personal matter that can be guided only by your own taste and the productions that are available, the type of audience to which it is addressed should be taken into consideration. Avoid presenting two features of a similar style or subject matter one after the other, as they will cancel each other out; alternate the documentary, the humorous and the poetic, and vary the lengths. If one production strikes you as particularly attractive or exciting, keep it for the end. If the order of the programme has been announced ahead and is not likely to be changed, it can help to copy the various sound-tracks in sequence on to one tape, avoiding the need to change reels during the show.

An entirely mechanical performance is lacking in personality, and I strongly recommend the addition of the human touch by personal presentation of the show from the front of the hall near the screen, before and in between the projections. Slide-tape is not yet as widespread as film, and a few words concerning the why and wherefore by the maker of the feature can be of interest to the audience. And this contact with the spectators will make them more friendly and indulgent in case of a breakdown.

DEALING WITH PROBLEMS

However careful you are, a breakdown is bound to take place sooner or later. When something goes wrong, do tell the audience what has happened. Nothing is more frustrating than to sit there wondering how long the interruption is going to last. If you have a microphone plugged in, stay by the projector and make a calm announcement asking the spectators to be patient for a few moments.

The most likely incidents are a blown-out projector bulb, a jammed slide and a break in the tape. Changing the bulb is a simple matter but may require some minutes of waiting for the old one to cool, if you are not to scorch your fingers. A jammed slide may take only a few seconds to clear; broken tape, fortunately a rare event, can be more awkward if part of it has become wound around the playing head. If it can be disentangled without damage, a quick join with cellulose tape will enable you to start up again.

The big problem which requires a rapid decision on your part is whether to go on where you left off when the breakdown took place, or to start that particular feature all over again. In most cases it is better to go back to the beginning. However, if it is a long production and you are over halfway (and can catch up on the synchronization) then just back up a little – say half a dozen slides – and continue. A mishap that should never happen but might, is that one of the transparencies has been placed in the wrong order. This can cause utter confusion. If they are manually projected, the only solution is to skip ahead one or two slides and wait for the sound to catch up. In the case of the fully automatic presentation, there is nothing to do but blush and hope that the audience will forgive you.

MAKE IT YOUR SHOW

The simplest presentation should give an impression of coherence. You owe this courtesy to the people who are to view it – just as you are obligated to them and to yourself to do the best you can by ruthlessly eliminating bad pictures and remaking the soundtrack if it was of poor quality the first time that you recorded it.

But apart from these basic essentials you can do what you like; it is your production and nobody else's. Even if you need assistance in taking the pictures, recording the tape or presenting the show, make sure that those who are helping you realize that they are doing just that and no more. It is the only way to obtain interesting results, both for yourself who will have the rewarding pleasure of expressing your personality in your work and for the spectators who, even though they may not agree with your outlook, will at least have been stimulated into some sort of reaction.

Developing the Theme

Considerably more colour film is taken during the months of July and August than in all the rest of the year put together. It is only when the daylight hours are numerous, and the great outdoors is calling, that in homes all over the country thoughts turn suddenly towards the camera which has been laid away for months, apart from a brief airing around Christmas time. Yet the lens of 35mm cameras is fast enough to operate in the dimmest light, and some modern colour emulsions are more sensitive than was the black-and-white stock of only a few years ago. The use of tape recorders is less seasonal, although it is likely that they could be employed much more. During the few days or weeks following their purchase, their owners record everything in the vicinity, but the excitement soon wears off.

Good cameras and tape recorders are expensive, and it is logical to try to get the most out of this investment. Audio-visual productions are more than just a means of expression or an agreeable pastime: they can help in everyday life (see page 108). In terms of creative pleasure however, our purpose is to discover how to keep the camera clicking and the recorder turning all through the year.

Let us presume that you have already made the most of your existing transparencies. You have selected a certain number, edited them, found some sort of an overall idea, added a few specially-taken pictures, recorded a soundtrack consisting of commentary, music and a few discreet effects – and so made one or two slide-tape features. That source is now dried up. The next production will have to be totally new, completely invented. Once again, the important ingredient is a theme; but this time, as you have no stock of slides as a background, the idea must come first. But where to find it?

IMPORTANCE OF SOUNDTRACK

It must be made quite clear from the start that a theme is not necessarily a plot. Some people brightly suggest that there are dozens of wonderful stories in the newspapers. This could conceivably be true for a maker of motion-pictures, and many cine clubs have been led along the dangerous path of melodramatic or would-be comic film plays by following that advice. But goodwill and keenness cannot replace professional talent, technique and above all experience. It is, however, somewhat less difficult to make a convincing sound recording, on the lines of a radio play, than to produce it visually; and one way of becoming a story-teller is to devise a form of presentation in which the text 'carries' the pictures, which illustrate it from time to time.

I realize that even to hint that in some cases the sound can be more important than the picture will be sufficient to condemn me as a heretic by the majority of the faithful photo and cine club members. I myself have been a movie-maker steadfast in my beliefs for so long that I wonder how I have managed to write such a phrase. Yet we must wake up to the fact that the precedence accorded to one part over the other is a relic of the early days. As films were for many years silent, they had to be made understandable by purely visual means, and their producers concentrated on the development of this aspect with very remarkable results. But we do not reject other forms of presentation because we admire the exciting editing of the Odessa steps sequence in *The Battleship Potemkin;* and, as our productions are *audio*-visual it is reasonable that they should give greater prominence to the sound.

One good example of this approach was provided by a slide-tape feature of a country village. The pictures were pleasant, but not more than that; it was the soundtrack that made the presentation memorable. An old man, seen outside his cottage, spoke the narration, or more exactly chatted about his life in the village, and the changes he had seen there. Occasionally, a few other voices were heard, but whether they were of the present or conjured up in his mind from the past one could not tell. A dog barked; a clock struck the hour. These few related sounds (I don't know whether they were recorded at the time or brought together afterwards by superimposition) captured a 'slice of life' that made a highly sensitive and personal work.

EXPANDING A THEME

Carrying to its limits the pre-eminence of the soundtrack, here are a few random thoughts on an up-to-date theme in which you can let yourself go, using numerous sound effects to conjure up that plague of the modern world: noise. Although the pictures are of secondary importance, they could provide a little light relief from the cacophony if humorously posed by the hero.

We first see him at a desk, trying to concentrate on his work. A roaring of cars is heard.

In the following slide, he is standing by the window that he has just closed; the traffic sounds diminish but a telephone rings. Close-up of him answering. A squeaky voice tells him it's a wrong number, as a noise of hammering is heard from the next room.

In the pub where he has gone for a drink to steady his nerves, a juke-box starts up. Out in the street, a pneumatic drill is ripping up the pavement. All the noises are jumbled together in a horrible mixture.

Comes a shot of a bottle of sleeping pills. Our hero is seen asleep. At last he is away from it all, and he dreams of the countryside. This is an excuse for a quiet, contrasting sequence: hills and dales, delicate music, a rippling stream, birdsong. The shrill ringing of the alarm-clock shatters it all. But he has taken a decision. He needs a rest, and will get away from town. By rail or by car – there is plenty of opportunity for noise in either case. Here he is in the village of his dreams. But nothing is as he imagined it. There is a TV set in his hotel, a sawmill by the rippling stream, motor bikes and tractors, and trippers everywhere with transistor radios. Even the unfamiliar country sounds are ear-shattering to a town-dweller: the cock crowing under his window at dawn, the cows lowing as they pass by, the horse and cart (at last, an opportunity to try out those empty coconut shells!)

I leave to your imagination the termination of this saga, whose purpose is merely to indicate how an idea can be expanded until it provides quite a quantity of material.

A THEME FOR VISUAL TREATMENT

As one word – in this case 'noise' – was enough to set off a train of thought, perhaps we can find another that will lead to a theme suitable for *visual* treatment.

As we are making use of colour slides, how about the spectrum itself? One of the colours: blue, for instance. Blue skies, or the deep blue sea. Blue moon. Feeling blue, singing the blues. Blue blood, blue stocking. Bluebells, bluebirds, Bluebeard's eighth wife.

Or how about an undoubted winner that will please everyone and enable you to take some striking close-ups: flowers. Let us jot down the mental pictures conjured up by this word.

Wild flowers in the fields, cornflowers and poppies, buttercups and daisies.
Spring flowers at the foot of the hills.
Peach and apple blossom.
A cottage 'with hollyhocks around the door'.
'When all at once I saw a crowd, a host of golden daffodils.'
'We'll gather lilacs in the Spring again.'
'The last rose of Summer,' 'To a wild rose,' 'Mighty like a rose.'
Not forgetting the Wars of the Roses.

And now people connected in some way with flowers.
The pretty girl plucking the petals of a marguerite as she murmurs: 'He loves me, he loves me not. . . . '
A street flower seller.

The retired gentleman with a pruning knife.
The elderly lady watering the flowers in pots on her window-sill.
Children with a posy for Mothers' Day.
A battle of flowers on the Riviera.

Flowers can even be symbols of sadness:
A wreath.
Dried flowers found in an old book.
Dead flowers taken from a vase.
Flowers drifting away on the water.

VARIATIONS ON A THEME

Visual themes can be interpreted in two ways: as a *progression,* where the idea unfolds towards its conclusion – the cinematic approach, which is the subject of the next chapter; or else as a *link* between images which may be very different in themselves, this latter being very suitable for slide-tape.

The films which Georges Méliès produced at the turn of the century were made like that. He was so happy and busy making use of the trick effects he had pioneered that he could not be expected to invent movie editing as well; in any case he saw no use for it. He owned a small theatre and his ideal was to reproduce on a grander scale the scenes he had imagined for the stage. It is an amusing game attempting to guess the theme which guides some of Méliès's films. I don't think it will be of much practical use to you, but just for fun try to imagine the title of the production that includes the following scenes: 1. Cain and Abel, 4000 B.C. 2. The Druids' Human Sacrifice, 500 B.C. 3. Nero and Slave Poisoning, A.D. 65. 6. The Gallows under Louis XI, A.D. 1475. 9. Modern Times, Street Fight, A.D. 1906. Described in his catalogue as 'one of the most artistic films ever made, in turn dramatic, pathetic, naturalist, satiric and ironic, very interesting all through', it was entitled *Civilisation Throughout the Ages*!

Less satirical and of more immediate use to us, but based on a similar linking together of disparate subjects, is the celebrated musical composition *Pictures at an Exhibition.* The strong and harmonious melodies of Moussorgsky admirably orchestrated by Ravel result in a unity of style so great that we are not in the least shocked to find a *Ballet of Chicks in their Shells* in the same context as the *Paris Catacombs* or the *Great Gate at Kiev*. At the beginning a *Promenade* sets the theme in which the viewer passes from one painting to another. Here is an interesting and simple idea which could well be developed, enabling you to use some slides which although fine photographs in their own right do not seem to fit in with others. Better yet, you could take some with such a series in mind, in the manner of a one-man show at an art gallery: portraits, still lifes, landscapes would all find their place in a sequence that would be agreeable to look at and owe nothing to the cinema, but on the contrary take advantage of the fact that the pictures are *not* moving.

USING PURELY PHOTOGRAPHIC THEMES

The link between pictures may on the other hand consist of similarities in the photographs themselves. Shots taken in fog or snow. Rain in town and country, reflecting in pools and wet pavements; or in gardens with a touch of autumn melancholy accompanied by Debussy's exquisite *Jardins sous la Pluie*. Night exposures of a modern city, presented in rapid sequence to a background of the final movement of Gershwin's *Concerto in F*. The Four Seasons motif, probably the most employed of all themes for scenics, is presumably still usable although timeworn, as it is always popular; but personally, if I hear Vivaldi's music with it again, I shall scream.

A succession of beautiful landscapes is a soothing balm to the weary mind. Unfortunately the mind is often soothed to sleep after a while, and a visual or auditory stimulant in small doses can be useful in keeping the audience alert. A striking effect that requires no technical skill is the 'comparison picture', two images of completely different subjects which nevertheless bear a common resemblance. A pocket-sized magazine published just before the War achieved considerable fame by using this method of satire, the photographs printed side by side usually being political figures in attitudes similar to those of birds and animals. Projected as slides, one after the other, the impact is the same.

The simplest pictures can be effective. I remember seeing at a French club a slide-series on London. It was rather banal and did not go much beyond such tourist attractions as Piccadilly Circus or the Tower; but two shots were so happily juxtaposed that they brought an 'Oh!' of pleasure from the audience, which they would not have done had they been presented separately. One was a low-angle shot of three red flowers in front of Buckingham Palace and the other showed three Guards in scarlet coats. When the transformation took place, both were raised to a height of interest that neither could have reached alone.

It so happened that these two slides were taken within a few minutes of each other, but we may observe such effects by comparing a recent picture with one made years before; hence the usefulness of a library of 'stock shots'.

TAKING A FRESH LOOK

A Londoner does not often spend his weekends taking photographs of Piccadilly Circus, any more than the Parisian spends *his* admiring the Eiffel Tower. It is not only because people have more time for their hobbies during the holiday period that so much more photography is undertaken in the summer months; it is because they feel that they must get away in order to find subject matter worthy of their attention. The simplest activity appears new and unusual when viewed under a different sky. In their own surroundings, they feel condemned to taking a few routine shots of family activities, for why should they want to record those streets, houses and shops that they see every day?

Yet the streets, houses and shops that we film with such enthusiasm in other countries are just as boring to their own inhabitants; we find them interesting because we see them from a different point of view. And Britain is just as strange to others as their land seems to us. For example, here is an excerpt from an introduction to England published by an American magazine under the title *Land of Bard and Beefeater*:

> 'Although England is roughly the size of the state of Alabama, it has a population about a fourth of the US, living among such picturesque scenery that the visitor is likely to find himself wondering if he's been turned loose in some story-book land, if not a region of movie sets filled with too-authentic-to-be-true props and backgrounds. Outside of London, England can be divided into three major geographical sections. Each is fully supplied with quaint villages and historical architecture. . . .'

To the Gallic eye, Britain appears not merely as a quaint and photogenic movie set, but as a land teeming with silent, inhibited natives. The following is translated from a guide-book issued by a French airline:

> 'In order to understand the British, you must try *not* to understand them. Just tell yourself that they are the opposite of what you had believed. They are tender and sentimental – but on condition that you are speaking to them of animals. Passionate, even exalted – on the subject of their traditions or their sports. And astonishingly demonstrative – when you have come to know that silence is their favourite means of communication. An Englishman knows how to make silences speak.'

Here, then, is a ready-made theme: suppose that your town is being seen for the first time by a visitor from Timbuctoo, Pernambuco, or – why not? – Uranus. As you escort him around, you will discover items of interest that you ignored or had forgotten. By taking a fresh look at everyday scenes, by imagining the comments made about them by someone to whom they are aspects of 'another world', your own senses will be sharpened. It is quite possible that you will end up with an evocation that will not only satisfy you, but will be of unusual interest to other members of your community.

The Cinematic Approach

To think in terms of cinema when dealing with slides may appear to be a frustrating exercise, but a background knowledge of the basic language of motion pictures is essential if we are to succeed in producing a certain type of feature. We do not have to limit ourselves to the linking together of differing elements, and it is quite possible to present a coherent story that unfolds towards a climax. The manner of the telling will not be that of a movie, but in the memory of the spectator the result may be much the same.

It is unfortunate that nobody has yet found a simple and easy name for slide-tape features. Obviously only the really keen can remember to use such a dreadful appellation, and even on the Continent, where *montage sonorisé* or *Diaporama* (see page 141) have a more pleasing sound, most people who do not actually make these productions refer to them as 'films'. There is no doubt that in the public mind they are confused with cinema. There is nothing new in this, for the point was already made many years ago.

ALEXANDER BLACK'S LANTERN SLIDES

The names of George Eastman and Thomas A. Edison are familiar to all, and it is only right that they should be mentioned here, because the first made it possible for everyone to take a photograph and the other was the inventor of a machine to record sound. But few people have heard of a third American called Alexander Black, who was ahead of his time and whose ideas were of particular interest to us.

He was one one of the first users of the Kodak camera, and the results he obtained were much admired by his artist friends, who suggested that he should print them as lantern slides for projection. Black did so, and showed them to numerous societies with increasing success. In 1893 – the very year that Edison was perfecting his Kinetoscope and two years before the Lumière brothers presented their celebrated performance of the Cinematograph – he wrote a little play centered on a young lady reporter who went around photographing interesting personalities. There were 250 slides altogether, which Black projected while simultaneously reading his dialogues. He explained that in certain sequences the background remained the same from shot to shot, but the figures were placed in different positions, so that they appeared to show progressive movement, though 'in a manner unlike that obtained by Mr. Edison'. It was not cinema, but it was not far from slide-tape.

It is strange to realise that even before the invention of cinema as we know it, someone was already wondering how to explain the way in which his presentations differed from motion pictures. This question seems to worry many people today, to such an extent that some of them are against the very principle of slide-tape merely because they cannot place it in a neat compartment either with cinema or with photography.

HOW MOVIES MOVE

There is of course no such thing as a *motion* picture. A film is composed of a series of still photographs known as frames, succeeding one another at the rate of 24 each second in professional sound films, 16 in silent films, and recently at a new speed of 18 frames a second for amateur productions using magnetic sound. The human eye does not discern the gap between the images, and the brain blends them together; it was the discovery of this natural phenomenon that led to the designing of early instruments bearing such wonderful names as *Zoetrope* and *Phenakistiscope* in which were placed little drawings of figures that seemed to run and hop about when viewed through revolving slits. This principle is the same that permits animated cartoons. Not everyone realizes this, as is shown by the story of the important lady visitor to the Walt Disney studios who, after a long and exhaustive trip through all the various departments finally turned to her host and said: 'That was very interesting, Mr. Disney. But tell me, just what makes Donald Duck move?'

Motion which in reality does not exist is imagined by the spectator from the series of static images presented to him. But his mind is capable of far more than this, and by the recall of events previously experienced, it can be satisfied by the mere suggestion of an idea or a scene. A total explanation is unnecessary, and can even be the cause of rapid lack of stimulation and therefore of loss of interest. This is very important to the cinematographer – and also to us, if we model our way of thinking on his.

EDITING IN THE CAMERA

The main problem facing every beginner with a cine camera is to know when to stop shooting. If, for example, he wishes to record a potter at work, he may well point the lens at him as he starts and continue to shoot as long as possible. As the scene has been recorded in the length of time that it happened, the projected result should be as interesting as the original; but in fact it will very likely seem far too slow. The spectator need only be shown the principal moments of the action, because although he has not seen that particular sequence before, he can remember others like it and is already imagining the action before it has happened. If, however, sections of the film are cut out in order to speed it up, the pot will appear to jerk and lurch about the screen, because the single shooting angle leaves the background stationary. It is more pleasing to have an idea of the layout of the pottery as well as a closer view of the making of the pot; the eyes of a visitor actually present would be moving constantly from one point to another and he would probably also move about the pottery. The movie-maker must therefore do the same by varying his 'taking' angle and perhaps using 'cutaway' shots of the surroundings.

In slide-tape you must think in a similar way. One photograph is not enough to cover a scene; it is necessary to take a series from different viewpoints. As the subject could be only a few inches away from the camera or as far away as the horizon, there are obviously an infinite number of distances available. But for practical purposes, such as the writing of a script, only five are used:

Long Shot (*LS*) This is a general view, embracing the entire landscape, building or room. Often taken with a wide-angle lens, it sets the scene, but the people and objects in it are too small to be recognizable.

Medium Long Shot (*MLS*) Could be the same as before, but taken with a normal lens. The action of the people in the scene is already clearer, if they are in the distance. If they come closer, the shot is a MLS as long as they can be seen 'from top to toe'.

Medium Close Up (*MCU*) This is considerably closer, and usually cuts people off at the waist. But it is still wide enough to permit certain other details of the background to be noticeable.

Close Up (*CU*) Says exactly what it means. A whole head filling the screen is a close-up, as is a bowl of fruit or a hand holding a knife.

Big Close Up (*BCU*) At this stage it is not the head that fills the screen but one eye, or one cherry. For this type of work, accessories are usually necessary to enable the camera to focus at such short range.

The classic method of taking a sequence is to begin with the LS and draw closer. This is logical and follows the natural course of things: if you are walking down the street and notice something of interest across the way, you approach it until you can see it in detail. For an instructional series, in which the subject matter is of prime importance, this is the best way to work. But the result is lacking in suspense, and it can often be more exciting to begin with a CU or even a BCU and only reveal its surroundings afterwards. If you saw *West Side Story* you will remember the opening sequence during which the screen was slowly covered by vertical streaks that gradually built up to form skyscrapers. This effect was not produced by changing the angle, but was based on the same idea of showing only a small part of the image at the start.

IMPACT AND MOVEMENT

The basic mistake made by all beginners in photography is to stand too far away from their subject. It is for this reason that the lens of fixed focal length fitted to many cine-cameras has a narrow angle of view (which results too often in the fearful 'hose-piping' indulged in by their owners who 'want to get everything in'!). Of course, when we find ourselves before a magnificent landscape or an enchanted castle, our reaction is also to get it all in. Unfortunately the reproduction rarely lives up to expectations, and landscapes in particular are nearly always disappointing unless they were taken under very favourable conditions of lighting. The reason is simply that one of the elements of the impact is missing: the sheer size of the scene is reduced to a projected image perhaps not more than three feet wide.

In an attempt to reconstitute this impression of grandeur, professional screens have become bigger and wider, but not everyone can install Cinerama in his living room. The simplest way for the amateur to inject some impact into his sequences is to make the most of close ups. A field of wheat compressed into the home screen is a nice picture, but a three-foot long grasshopper on a blade of grass is a sight to make you sit up. And an audience must be made to sit up occasionally.

It cannot be repeated too often that a succession of images that are merely beautiful, technically perfect and well composed has a soporific effect on the keenest of spectators. There are, of course, people who agree with this contention when it is applied to a motion picture, yet are against it when the images referred to are slides. It is a curious fact that many amateur film makers who are willing to spend a small fortune on film stock in order to produce 'dramatic' productions which, alas, generally miss the mark (it has even been known for otherwise perfectly sane families to invent and act out gruesome accidents to pep up their holiday movies) become indignant if one suggests that a series of colour transparencies can be presented in a manner which is not smooth, syrupy and dull. To these fanatics, slides cannot be exciting or stimulating, because – as they are fond of repeating – slides do not move.

In fact, slides *can* move in the only sense of the word that really matters – by moving the audience emotionally. How many amateur *films* move, according to both meanings? I have sat through miles of film in which the producer, desperately aware that he was using a cine camera for a subject that did not warrant it, panned and tilted and zoomed in an attempt to bring life and action to the screen. They recalled a critic's comments on the first cinematograph show in 1895: 'Indeed there was movement . . . the very mountains danced!' I wish I could say that I have been moved very often by the best amateur films (those shown at festivals are presumably the best, and I have attended many, on both sides of the Channel). But one of the most exciting amateur productions I can recall – how I wish I had made it – shown at the Vichy Festival before an enthusiastic audience of 600 people was not a film at all; it was a slide sequence presented by dual-projection.

Nevertheless, if it is true that nothing is quite so futile as an amateur movie trying to ape Hollywood – and a Hollywood of the 1930's, at that – it is equally true that it does not have to limit itself to a straightforward narrative style. It can set out to move its audience and succeed, and the slide-tape feature can achieve the same power and intensity by using identical means, because those means are not necessarily allied to motion.

It has been said that action can be thought of as the *thing* that is done, and movement as *how* it is done. As we can only make use of one of these two elements, the imagination of the spectator has to provide the other; his reaction depends on the manner, and in particular the order, in which the images are presented to him.

CREATING A MOOD

The principal ways of creating a certain atmosphere or mood in an audio-visual production are, in the audio part, the style of the text–poetic or factual, personal or detached; the voice and delivery of the narrator; the type of music and use of effects. These are the subject of the next chapter.

The visual part is influenced by the colour of the shots; their composition; the rhythm of their passage (i.e. the length of time that each stays on the screen); and, perhaps most important of all, the order of their editing. We have already dealt with the different effects obtained by bright or subdued colours, and the possibility of arranging them in a form of progression. The composition of the shot is allied to this, but concerns more particularly the placing of the subject within the area of the frame. When the hero and heroine are in a close-up embrace, the proximity of the camera not only enables the audience to appreciate every detail of the kiss, but also by filling the entire screen with their heads, it symbolizes the fact that they, and they alone, are of importance to each other at that moment, the rest of the universe being eliminated. But as they walk away hand in hand into the sunset, the camera moves back, and these two figures are soon dominated by the landscape: the outside world is taking over once again.

The so-called rules of composition are often ignored by today's photographers, but they can still be of use in setting a mood, if only subconsciously. The most ardent nonconformist cannot prevent horizontal lines from giving a peaceful impression, diagonal lines suggesting drive and thrust, or vertical lines from being lofty and inspirational; but he could accentuate a situation of conflict, for instance, by deliberately composing the picture in an unusual manner – perhaps with a person too close to the edge, or looking out of the screen instead of into it. A feeling of dullness and respectability is increased by placing the subject in the dead centre of the image, and doing the same with the horizon, which, as everyone knows, is supposed never to bisect the space but should be not more than a third up or a third down.

CREATIVE EDITING

It is no exaggeration to say that editing is the most vital phase in the making of a film or a slide-tape feature. The movement created by the relationship between images was regarded by the Russians as the most distinctive quality of film. In their eyes, it was the possibility of arranging and re-arranging the shots, of leaving them on the screen for a longer or shorter time, that constituted the art of the cinema and transformed a mere method of mechanical representation into an exciting means of expression. Pudovkin felt that the strips of celluloid coming straight from the camera were dead things which acquired life and movement only when a significant relationship was established between them during editing.

Another director, Koulechov, set out to demonstrate this by an experiment that has remained famous. He took a lengthy close-up of an actor, telling him to show no particular emotion but only to gaze with some intensity out of the picture. He then cut the film into separate pieces, and in between each section placed a shot of a completely different subject: a beautiful woman, a laden table, a funeral. Projecting the sequence before an audience, he asked the spectators their opinion of the actor's ability. All were impressed by his emotional response to the various scenes, remarking that he had expressed in turn desire, hunger and sadness with great skill. But of course they were attributing to him the reactions that they had felt themselves.

Editing can do even more than this. When placed in a certain

Effective editing. 1 – The Coward. On a romantic hilltop, Johnny X is gazing into the fabulously blue eyes of Mary Y.

Mary Y suddenly notices –

– the villainous Z approaching.

Z looks threateningly at the couple.

Johnny X runs off, leaving Mary Y to her fate.

Mary Y screams as Z comes closer.

Effective editing. 2 – The Hero. Mary Y, out for a stroll on a romantic hilltop, suddenly sees –

– the villainous Z standing threateningly before her.

Mary Y screams for help.

Johnny X, who has heard her cry, runs to her aid.

Z moves away, muttering imprecations.

Mary Y gazes with admiration into the fabulously brown eyes of her saviour.

order, a series of shots has a definite meaning, yet by re-arrangement the same images can be made to express exactly the opposite. In unscrupulous hands this may lead to the worst forms of distortion, as was proved by some of the Nazi propaganda films made during World War II. Although the images were of actual events, they were edited in a manner that made them appear to illustrate a fallacious commentary.

SLIDE-TAPE AND COMIC-STRIP

The slide sequence here may remind you of the way the story is told in the newspaper comic strip. There is much to be learned by studying the technique of these strips. Sociologists tell us that this art-form is almost as important to the modern world as the cinema and TV, and that 80 per cent of newspaper readers turn to the comics page before looking at anything else. This is not surprising, if we consider that the ancient Egyptians were already fond of picture stories – sufficiently so to have them painted on the walls of their tombs.

In comic strips as in slide-tape, the attention is divided between the image and the text, and the main problem is to know how much importance to give to each. In Egyptian times, precedence was sometimes given to the illustrations and sometimes to the hieroglyphs, but even when the latter predominated they were always artistically composed as a part of the entire layout. In mediaeval times the drawings were usually ornaments to the narrative, which was deemed more important in view of the ancient principle that the written word was the key to civilization.

Authors of comic strips share one great advantage with the amateur slide-tape producer: they can ignore the critics and write directly for their audience, while developing their own personal ideas. This relative freedom has enabled cartoonists to work out some very interesting solutions to the problems of the medium, especially as regards the balance between image and text. The dialogue is reduced to essentials, and sometimes replaced by visual symbols: the light-bulb meaning 'I have an idea', the saw in a log that represents a snoring sleeper – and of course the fabulous collection of noises imitated by invented words, the VROOMS, GLOPS and R-R-R-RINGS. In this wonderful world, sound and picture are inextricably mixed.

COMIC-STRIP AND CINEMA

Many film directors are interested in comics, and make collections of them. Fellini is reported to have said that the adventures of Dick

Tracy were 'a hundred times more beautiful than the best American gangster films'. There is no doubt that some cartoons are not only inventive but extremely well planned and laid out. Outstanding in their particular field are Prince Valiant, whose elegant style is a perfect setting for tales of chivalry, and Tarzan, in which the backgrounds are a blend of the expressionist school of painting and oriental art. Chester Gould and Milton Caniff can be said to have pioneered the cinematic approach to cartooning, assembling a succession of peak moments that give an impression of movement. The montage is identical to cinema; the dialogue can be part of the scene or narrated 'off' by an invisible commentator. In recent years, all the photographic effects have been adopted by certain cartoonists: low and high angle shots, silhouetted backgrounds, even exaggerated perspective as seen through extra-wide-angle lenses. Zooming is sometimes copied by increasingly closer views of the same object.

This adaptation of cinema technique by graphic artists is only one example of the way in which the artificial barriers that had been set up between various media are collapsing. Theatre, ballet and opera now blend together to present 'total spectacles' that may also make use of projections; open-air productions combine recorded stereophonic sound, lighting effects and live actors; and television does not hesitate to adopt any method which is suitable to its need of the moment.

The professional is discovering a new freedom of expression, but it is the amateur, strangely enough, who remains hidebound by conventions all the more absurd because they are unnecessary. Although he likes to repeat that he is not tied down by commercial considerations, the results he obtains are often only pale copies of the work of those who *are* so restricted.

Yet if the amateur who, by definition, creates only *for love* of his art, should really want to try out new styles of audio-visual presentation – who is to stop him?

The Soundtrack

Basically, there are three types of soundtrack, normally all used together, but sometimes separately: commentary, music and effects (the latter recorded live or copied from a disc). Let us take them in turn.

SETTING THE COMMENTARY STYLE

Understandably, the writing of a commentary is to many people the most difficult part in the making of a slide-tape feature. Its importance cannot be over-emphasized, for the most splendid series of pictures can be ruined by a clumsily-worded or badly-spoken narration. On the other hand, it can happen that a fairly ordinary collection of visuals is transformed into a memorable presentation by its soundtrack. Unfortunately there can be no hard and fast rules, as each production is the expression of its maker's own personality. However, before giving some general hints, here is a short list of *don'ts* for script-writers and narrators.

1. *Don't* describe the picture: remember that in itself it is supposed to be worth a thousand words! Of course the text must have a relation to the image, but it should merely add a little information – or set a mood – that is not apparent.
2. *Don't* on the other hand, mention something that should be visible but is not. In one production. the narrator became quite excited about a 'very colourful market' which was held in a certain town. But the picture showed the market-place deserted, because the photographer had passed through on the wrong day. The audience naturally felt let down.
3. *Don't* be over-enthusiastic: If a scene is beautiful, the slide should show it, and there is no point in gilding the lily by lyrical exclamations about 'exquisite stained glass' or 'superb architecture'.
4. *Don't* forget that your script is meant to be spoken and not read. If it is too polished it can sound pedantic. Read it aloud a few times before recording it, and if it does not sound natural, change it. One or two repetitions and even hesitations are more agreeable to the ear than high-flown and stilted language.
5. *Don't* go overboard the other way, though. Unless there is a good reason for them, ejaculations and familiarity can be just as irritating.

And do beware of clichés: 'As the sun sinks low in the west, and our ship draws away from the shore, we reluctantly say Farewell to romantic Ulah-Ulah. . . .' This sentence, which accompanied so many glorious Technicolor sunsets in a series of 'Traveltalks' widely shown in the late 1930's has now become a classic of corn.

To the maker of slide-tape features, however, it is no laughing matter, for he is faced with the same problem as was Mr. James Fitzpatrick. Just what are you going to say? Even in the case of a travelogue, the time to think about it is before taking the slides, before beginning the holiday that will be the reason for it all. When you have decided on the form that your commentary is to take, you will be better able to select the scenes you wish to take, and especially those that you will not photograph.

As you probably have not seen the place you are planning to visit and are certainly not intending to follow a script while enjoying your holiday, you may wonder how it can be possible to write a commentary in advance, even if you are surrounded by stacks of travel brochures and guide books. But please note that I said 'the form' that it will take. In other words, although you cannot know what you will be describing, it is wise to have an idea of the manner in which you will be presenting it.

As an example, let us suppose that on a journey through France you have stopped at the Palace of Fontainebleau, and taken a shot or two of its famous carp pond. Basically, there are three ways of commenting them:

1. *Guidebook style:* Originally built as a hunting lodge in the 12th Century, the Palace of Fontainebleau first knew splendour under King Francis the First, who in 1526 . . .
2. *Family Scrapbook:* Peter and Jane were looking at the fish in this pond when Jane slipped and nearly fell in the water, but luckily Peter . . .
3. *Flight of Poesy:* As we gaze on this magnificent palace, are we not tempted to echo the immortal words of Keats: 'Much have I travell'd in the realms of gold . . .'

EFFECT OF STYLE ON PHOTOGRAPHS

It might seem that an equal dose of one-third of each of these styles would add up to a well-balanced narration, but in fact it would be very difficult to blend them into a coherent whole. Also, as certain people have a natural tendency to be gay or sad or romantic and this is reflected in their speech or manner of writing, it is as well to make the most of this right from the start. A point of view – whether right or wrong – makes for purposeful narration and consequently for interesting productions.

The choice of style affects the actual photographs you will take. Generally, some facts are necessary, but they rapidly become boring and few people really care whether a particular Gothic spire was built in 1476 or 1485. However if you really like architecture and history, or plan to use the pictures for educational purposes, the guidebook style may be acceptable. Your photographs will concentrate on certain specialised aspects, while shots of the children skylarking about will be limited, or at least not used in that particular production.

Most cameras are purchased to photograph the family: shots of them taken against novel backgrounds are the backbone of holiday slides. But funny stories about vacation escapades can soon become stale and should not be attempted on a recorded soundtrack unless a really talented speaker can be found. If this miracle does happen, a light-hearted approach is well worthwhile, but it must be reflected in the pictures themselves.

The world's greatest comedian would have a hard time trying to make cheerful comments on long-shots of landscapes with the family doggedly staring into the lens or at the horizon. A brisk series concentrating on enjoyable moments, with only enough background to set the scene, is needed.

If you do not have a bouncy family and are given to romantic dreaming, then the poetic style is for you. Great emotional impact can come from the potent mixture of words and images. We are not all poets: but there are many beautiful poems in the English language, some of which conjure up a ready-made visual interpretation. But beware! You are inviting ridicule if the slides are not perfect. The photography and editing must be of top quality, for nothing is more grotesque than a rolling, majestic soundtrack backing up hastily-taken, badly-composed images. This is the style for the holiday-maker with plenty of time, who does not mind waiting for the light to be in the right place.

It is also the ideal production for a sunset ending. A colourful sky is irresistible and you are bound to have taken one. You could try to be original and place it in the middle, but your guests will think the show is ending when they see it and start shuffling about, and will give a gasp when a daylight scene follows, accompanied by the words: 'The next day, we left for . . . .' So the sunset over the ocean must go back at the end where it belongs – or at least near the end if there should be some time-exposure night scenes for the ultimate conclusion.

Finally, if you do not read your own commentary, should it be read by a man or a woman? Without wishing to be unkind, it must be admitted that nine times out of ten a male voice is to be preferred. For one thing it is easier to record than the female voice, which is often too highly pitched. However, in the lucky event of a pleasing contralto being available, it is very suitable for certain subjects of a poetic type. And it can be interesting to have both a man and a woman reading the text alternately.

LINKING SLIDE AND COMMENTARY

With the poetic style of presentation, mood is more important than precise details, and the slides and commentary do not have to coincide exactly. The narration and music can flow on at a normal pace; the pictures are changed at appropriate moments. But in the more frequent travelogue-type of feature, the text is usually descriptive and must fall on the image that concerns it. As each slide requires at least a few seconds of screen time, the manner the most often adopted is to write a phrase or two for each one. For example, let us imagine a shopping expedition in a North African bazaar: we have seen various longshots of the alleyways, now come three closer views of the articles on sale. This is how a standard one-paragraph, one-slide commentary for these three close-ups could sound:

Leather goods: In these Arab bazaars, the most sought-after souvenirs among the tourists are the ever-popular baboosh or pointed slippers.

Metalwork: Exquisitely chased metalwork is a great temptation for those with a little more money to spend.

Jewellery: To many of the ladies, a dazzling display of colourful stones in curious settings is the strongest attraction.

And so on: one picture, one sentence, change the slide, one sentence. . . . If this method is employed throughout the whole production, it becomes almost unbearably monotonous. In the hope of improving matters, one could modify the text:

Leather goods: As they wander through the bazaar admiring the various stalls, the tourists are tempted by colourful displays of local craftsmanship, in particular attractive slippers –

Metalwork: chased metalwork –

Jewellery: and jewellery.

The trouble now is that the three descriptive words succeed one another, and as there is a slide for each, the narrator will be obliged to leave a gap of a few seconds for the images to be seen. But the phrase should be spoken continuously if it is to sound normal or even be understood, so the result will be worse than before.

A better solution is to adapt the one-slide, one sentence style in such a way that the change of picture does not take place in between the phrases but in the course of a sentence. This makes the presentation more difficult for the projectionist if he is 'playing it by ear' without a synchronizer, but considerably less tedious for the audience.

Leather goods:	As they wander through the bazaar, some tourists are attracted by displays of handmade leather goods, in particular these typical pointed slippers. Others are tempted by a neighbouring stall
Metalwork:	where they can admire exquisitively chased metalwork. The ladies may protest that it is too cumbersome to carry home, but the true reason for this lack of enthusiasm is probably that they would prefer
Jewellery:	to be offered a colourful stone set in a curious mount that is said to bring good luck.

As the pictures are really self-explanatory it may not be considered necessary to describe them at all. The sequence could be introduced during the previous general shots of the alleyways by a phrase such as 'The tourists wandered happily through the bazaar, admiring the attractive displays', and then evocative music would take over to provide an atmospheric background. A well-balanced soundtrack usually contains a mixture of all these methods.

UNCONVENTIONAL FORMS OF NARRATION

Most commentaries are of a safe, neutral style, spoken by an impartial observer. It is sometimes more interesting to adopt a personal manner.

DIRECT ADDRESS

The narrator, who should have some experience of storytelling or public speaking (but not be too hearty), talks to the audience in a conversational tone: 'By the way, did you know that it takes a ton of petals to make only ten ounces of oil of roses?' or 'Have you ever seen the Taj Mahal by moonlight?'

THE SUBJECT ITSELF

A monologue in which an animal or an inanimate object speaks about itself: 'I am the locomotive of the 8.45 train to London, and each morning as I rush through the countryside. . . .' 'My name is Spot. I am a little mongrel dog and my mistress is Mary Jane.' This should not be taken too seriously, as it can easily become embarrassingly maudlin.

SEVERAL VOICES

An amusing variation on the above is Michael Tickner's Audioscope production *Crazy Creatures,* a light-hearted stroll through the animal kingdom, enlivened by strange and comical comments by the animals themselves. The talent of Ernest Burden who recorded all the voices plays a great part in its success. In my own slide-tape feature *Standing Room Only* (see page 156), the statues in a French park voice their opinions of life and of each other; in this case the soundtrack was recorded by three people.

AD-LIB

Unrehearsed conversations or interviews recorded on a portable machine can occasionally be used after careful editing. One interesting documentary was on the dying craft of seaweed collection, accompanied by the comments of a Breton fisherman being interviewed by the photographer. Both voices were retained, but it might have been preferable to cut out the questions entirely, leaving only a monologue.

POSTCARDS FROM ABROAD

Once very popular in the world of amateur cinema, this style is used for travelogues. Each sequence begins with a picture-postcard from that particular place, and the commentary is in the form of a letter: 'Dear Margaret, We are now in Paris, and I am writing this at the terrace of a café on the Champs-Elysées. . . .' For some reason that I am unable to explain, a feminine voice is usually considered necessary for the epistolatory style.

AVAILABILITY OF MUSIC

Slide-tape features with no commentary at all are very attractive on condition that they have form and meaning. Sequences based on themes by the Impressionist composers (Debussy, Delius, Ravel) are an excellent though perhaps rather obvious example. A short, well-known work or even a popular song makes a good feature if it forms the main theme, but very familiar music should never be used merely as a background to commentary, even though it might seem appropriate, for it is apt to be distracting. Records of 'mood music' are available, offering a wide selection ranging from 'family picnic' through 'foreboding' to what was once called 'teashop pretty-pretty'. Most of them are rather short, but this is not always a drawback. You will have to be guided by your personal taste and the style of the production, and as just about every composition both ancient and modern has been recorded on disc, the choice is as vast as the musical field itself.

MUSICAL UNDERSTATEMENT

To the modern cinemagoer and television viewer accustomed to elaborately scored film music, the pianist of the silent era appears a rather comical figure. Yet his single instrument added greatly to the enjoyment of the early productions, and some of those lone players were artists in their particular genre. Probably in reaction to the torrents of syrupy orchestral compositions poured under and over so many motion-picture epics, some directors in recent years have rediscovered the value of musical understatement. The classic example, still remembered today, is *The Third Man,* wherein Sir Carol Reed made use of a solitary zither. The strange atmosphere of René Clément's *Forbidden Games* was underlined by two guitars playing a melody adapted from a 16th century work. Other films have employed only two or three instruments.

If only for reasons of economy, this simplified approach seems ideal for the amateur slide-tape enthusiast who, with a little talent and imagination, could produce unusual soundtracks which would have the added advantage of being entirely original. Just as the zither evoked Vienna, so the instruments used should have some relation with the atmosphere of the presentation. Drums can be menacing – or of course military; flute and harp (a delightful combination) conjure up lyrical landscapes; and in some cases a small jazz or 'pop' group is perfectly suitable.

MUSIQUE CONCRÈTE

Many people find it hard to assimilate contemporary music, and in particular *musique concrète* and other electronic mixtures. Admittedly it is rarely 'pleasing' to the ear when listened to in a concert hall, and often has an undertone of menace. But when used as an accompaniment it can be remarkably effective, not only in conjunction with modern subjects but even with more hackneyed themes, to which it adds an exciting new dimension.

EFFECTIVE SOUNDS

We have seen that sound effects are most entertaining to create and record, but we must be careful not to make use of them too often or in the wrong place. Now that it has become fairly simple for amateur moviemakers to add sound to their films, many of them, thrilled by this opportunity, introduce effects whether they are necessary or not. Travelogues are inundated with them: no Swiss cow without its bell, no ship without a siren, no river scene without an outboard motor. In certain cases, unfortunately, the result obtained by the producer is the opposite of his intention; instead of adding to the realism of the rendering, these effects stand out by their obvious artificiality. Unless a sound effect can bring some new atmosphere that could not be felt without it, its use resembles the type of commentary which explains everything the pictures are showing.

It is important to differentiate the *general* sounds from the *particular* which point out a specific action or mechanism. It is the latter, often introduced too loudly and abruptly, that break the continuity. On the other hand the *general,* which are large and vague sounds such as wind, waves, crowd noises, traffic and the ever-popular seagulls are most useful when utilized with discretion, and being of indeterminate length they can be mixed in with music or faded in and out at will.

These remarks apply equally to cinema and to slide-tape, although when the picture is static the approach, oddly enough, can be more free. In some cases, the very stillness of the image is a quality in itself. The best movie image vibrates and shimmers a little, the whir of the projector is often a distraction. But the silence and fixity of a slide can have an almost hypnotic effect in a given context. In one French prize-winning production about Nohant, the country home of George Sand, we were shown around the estate to the accompaniment of excerpts from the author's novels. When we had absorbed the mood, the commentary stopped, the faint musical background ceased. On the screen, a shot of the house. Out of the silence the only recorded sound – the song of a bird, clear and sharp. I have never forgotten the extraordinary effect of this suspended moment of time.

I must add that this particular feature was presented by dual projection (see page 114). This effect would perhaps be more difficult to achieve with normal slide changing methods.

The soundtrack can transform the most banal sequence, and a certain amount of 'cheating' in the presentation has great possibilities. Suppose we have a shot of a child crying against an unidentifiable background such as a sky. During the projection of this shot, the sound of waves is heard. Audience reaction? She is crying because she is frightened of the sea and does not want to bathe. And suppose we play a recording of cannon-fire instead – what horrors can we not conjure up?

The field of soundtrack recording is a very wide one, with plenty of room for imaginative exploration.

The Audio-Visual in Education

We have now discussed just about all the technical aspects of slide-tape as presented in the 'classic' manner, that is to say with one projector, and the time has almost come to progress to the next and most exciting stage, dual-projection. But to do so immediately, without considering two very important applications of these audio-visual productions, would give the impression that their only purpose is creative satisfaction for oneself and an agreeable entertainment for others. To think of slide-tape only as a source of pleasure is to underestimate its usefulness and possibilities. Each day, this medium brings a greater contribution to the fields of education and business.

Its role in the world of commerce and affairs (the subject of the next chapter) is yet to be fully developed; on the other hand, professionally-produced visual aids are more and more employed in schools, and the slide projector and tape recorder are now standard equipment there. But are they being put to the fullest possible use? Not only as an aid to teaching – where 'home-made' presentations can in many cases give more fruitful results than generalized filmstrips intended for a wider circulation – but also to keep a record of past achievements and to form a link with parents and visitors?

AUDIO-VISUALS AS TEACHING AIDS

It has often been said that the twentieth century is the century of the image. Willingly or not, in the streets and in our homes, we are constantly saturated with pictures. Children are exposed to them even before going to kindergarten, not only in their picture books but also by means of family photographs, or cinema and television. There is no escape from them. This fact, which has become one of the most important problems of our time, interests all those who are in some way involved in education. The development of pictorial representation in teaching is proceeding at a fantastic speed, although its origins may be traced back to the dawn of humanity.

EARLY VISUAL AIDS

The pictures that primitive man drew on the walls of his caves with rudimentary tools and colours were reproductions of the phenomena which surrounded him and representations of imaginary beings. Some people, remarking on the carefully indicated position of an archer bending his bow, or of an arrow striking the mammoth in a fatal spot, like to see in these drawings a form of teaching aid; but it seems that practical demonstration would have been more likely among these hunters.

Mediaeval Christianity made use of frescoes and sculptures in churches as giant picture stories of the lives of the saints and as an education in morality, with striking examples of punishment in Hell and reward in Heaven. These were not only forceful lessons but often admirable works of art; but as they were unique they could be seen only by a limited number of people.

With the coming of printing, pictures left the sanctuary for the street. Then they entered school in the year 1685, when the first educational 'visual aid', an illustrated book for children, was completed by John Amos Comenius. His *Orbis Sensualium Pictus* (The World of the Senses) combined engravings with text.

In the nineteenth century, J. Pestaloz and F. Froebel stressed the necessity for appealing to all the physical senses, and photographs appeared more and more in printed material. 'Photography is life' became a fashionable phrase, and the magic-lantern entered college. Visual projection devices were really put into extensive use during World War II, when the rapid training of large groups of men and women with dissimilar educational backgrounds became essential, and it was soon evident that the printed page alone was inadequate.

The evolution of sound images has been different, because until very recent times there was no possibility of conserving them. We have in some cases the manuscripts of speeches made by the great orators of the past, but their voices are lost, as are those of the famous men who created history. And although music can be written down, its exact quality can never be rediscovered, for it depends on the talent and the temperament of the musician who interprets it. No music is twice the same, no speech ever expressed in a similar manner.

Since the invention of the phonograph, progress has been rapid, and modern technique is amazing. The teacher now has at his disposal all the means of sound and picture reproduction that he can desire. But in certain branches of education, acceptance of this form of communication has been slow when compared with its rapid advance in other fields of activity.

It is only necessary to recall the extraordinary battles of wits that had to be fought, sometimes for years on end, by educators in some European schools in order to triumph over ancient rules and regulations and so introduce simple and inexpensive aids to teaching such as blackboards, to realise the negative reactions provoked by the first attempts at 'cultural mechanisation'. Many masters felt that to bring to their class the sounds and images of all the world might be of benefit to some pupils, but only a source of confusion to others. Certainly audio-visual aids are not a cure-all for teachers or for students, and it is important to make use of them in a logical manner. Their effectiveness depends on the way in which they are integrated into the general lesson.

INTEGRATING AUDIO-VISUALS INTO LESSONS

Some teachers consider slide-series or films as mere illustrations to their lesson. They make use of them after a verbal description if they consider that the words do not give a sufficiently vivid impression of the subject. But in the mind of such masters, the image plays only a secondary or even superfluous role. They may well say to their pupils at the end of the period: 'I would have liked to show you some photographs, but there wasn't time' – thus proving that these were not an essential part of the lesson. They look on projection as a moment of recreation and relaxation offered to the students after the serious work has taken place. Despite the ever-growing recognition of the utility of audio-visual aids by educational authorities, the idea that they are a sort of show or spectacle tagged on to the curriculum is still widespread today.

The ideal way to make use of slide projection, sound recording and films would be to integrate them totally into the class or discussion, by considering them as an irreplaceable intermediary to knowledge of the outside world. The modern child, it is said, 'only recognizes things that he has already seen in pictures'. Consequently, starting from a basis of images that remind him of known objects or phenomena, the teacher should lead his pupil towards those as yet unknown. Used in this manner, the picture or sound recording would be incorporated into the lesson at specific moments prepared by the master, and be under his absolute control.

It must be admitted that this ideal is difficult to realise, and that the teacher often has to stand by while a motion-picture film or a television set takes over his task. His pupils, already conditioned to a stereotyped form of thinking by the radio and TV programmes to which all are simultaneously subjected in their homes, continue passively to absorb the flow of pictures and sounds. Many teaching aids are of a standardized nature to be be used in many differing classes and contain elements that do not interest a specific group.

To offset this danger, the teacher can utilize to the maximum the slide-tape features made by himself and his students. The active learning involved in the creation of the materials is very satisfying to the participants and serves as a valuable stimulus. Fortunately, the present trend is to greater use and increase of interest in amateur photography and tape recording, allied to the particular techniques needed for the preparation of such productions. As surveys in the

United States suggest that by the time a primary grade child of today reaches the age of 30 he may be using visual communication more than he does the medium of print, he may as well become acquainted with it as early as possible.

SUITABILITY FOR YOUNGER PUPILS

Even the smallest children love to take part in producing their own audio-visual programme. Incredible though it may seem, a project organized by the Toronto Board of Education enabled a group of seven-year-olds of a Canadian city to make their own movie, using a simple Super-8 camera. They even added a commentary afterwards, using the classroom tape recorder. A report on this apparently very successful venture stated that the children showed an ability and self-confidence which few adults could emulate. If they were able to master the greater difficulties of film-making, there is no reason why others of that age should not be able to take still photographs and present them in sequence with a soundtrack.

Photographs of drawings and paintings by the very youngest children make delightful slides, and their own comments (preferably recorded unawares to them) form a fascinating accompaniment.

PHOTOGRAPHING PAINTINGS AND DRAWINGS

In this case, the teacher will presumably take the slides, and his task is simplified if he uses a reflex-type camera, because at short range he may have problems in centering through a separate viewfinder. Fixed-focus cameras need a 'portrait' attachment. The simplest and most even form of lighting is daylight and bright sunshine brings out the colours most vividly. In the shade, the pictures take on a bluish cast; on a dull day they are more subdued in hue.

The camera can be set up on a tripod with ball-and-socket head, facing a drawing board set on an easel. The drawings are fixed to the board with cellulose tape; paintings are merely placed on the easel. The camera must of course be quite parallel to the board, and inclined at a similar angle. The sun should not be directly behind the camera, not only because of the problem of shadows cast on the easel by the apparatus, but especially because direct light may reflect back from the drawing or painting into the lens; it is preferable for the light to come slightly from the side.

A similar set-up can be used indoors, but the illumination is less simple. If two floodlamps of equal wattage are available, one should be set up on either side of the painting. They must be carefully shaded from the lens, and artificial-light type film is required. Electronic flash is not very suitable: with only one flash-head the lighting is uneven, and even with an extension head on the other side the colour rendering may not be too satisfactory. It is always a wise precaution to use a cable release, because at close range even a minute vibration of the camera when operating the shutter can cause unsharpness.

It may be possible to use the paintings as the basis for a little story, in which case the slides should not be limited to 'one painting, one shot'. Two or three closer views of certain portions can be taken (if the camera has extension tubes or close-up lenses) to follow or precede the entire picture. The opposite method can also be adopted, the children being asked to illustrate a story. Short tales with plenty of dialogue can be taped by the children themselves, and a little music and effects added for atmosphere; the slides being taken afterwards according to the necessities of the script.

PROJECTS FOR OLDER PUPILS

During holidays, older children and their parents take slides of resorts at home or countries abroad; an interesting group project is one that enables it to edit these pictures into orderly sequences and then write and record a commentary, with an appropriate musical background sought out by the students themselves.

In the United States, pupils and local educators join in sending a series of taped messages to students in various countries who, in turn, send them recordings. This project not only creates interest, but encourages the pupils to study geography, history and literature. The fact that there are actual people speaking to one another lends a human touch to the proceedings. It would be a simple matter to carry such experiences a step further by including in the package visual material in the form of slides to accompany the tapes; for posting, these could be removed from their mounts and placed in light transparent folders numbered in sequence.

AN INTERNATIONAL PRODUCTION

A rewarding experience in which I participated took place near Paris when the French Ministry of Youth and Sports organized a 10-day seminar for 36 students from six different nations, who had come to perfect their knowledge of the way of life of the region, as well as its historical background. Soon after their arrival I was invited to give a talk on the technique and possibilities of slide-tape, illustrated by two productions I had made in the locality.

On the evening of their final session I returned as a guest at the farewell reception, during which, to my agreeable surprise, the students presented a slide-tape feature that they had produced entirely by themselves during the week. In view of the short time at their disposal they had made it in black-and-white, developing the film in the darkroom of the Youth Centre and printing the selected shots on positive film.

They told me afterwards that the soundtrack had been completed barely half-an-hour before the show – but nevertheless they had managed to pack into its 15 min considerable humour and an admirable synthesis of what they had learned during their stay. The official representatives of the Ministry and the Municipality were delighted to be shown in such a pleasant manner the concrete results of this international gathering, and the students found that the desire to make an audio-visual production had given purpose and direction to their research.

GUIDE FOR PARENTS AND VISITORS

Plenty of otherwise dull meetings would be enlivened and enriched by a slide-tape feature replacing boring explanations and sets of figures by images and sounds that recreate for parents the activities of their children. Certain schools occasionally attempt a motion picture of this type, but the sheer expense and technical difficulty of film production make it a hazardous and lengthy project. Interior cinematography in large rooms involves complex lighting, whereas with a still camera, a brief time-exposure or flash can be sufficient. A film requires visual continuity and even acting talent from the participants. A 30-min recorded visit of a school, utilizing transparencies taken at various convenient moments and backed up by an attractive soundtrack (the making of which is in itself a fascinating exercise for the pupils) would require about 150 slides and a roll of tape. Think of the complication and cost of a sound film lasting half an hour!

TRAINING AIDS

In certain visual training aids demonstrating techniques such as handicrafts, movies can give too rapid an impression; the various stages are more easily assimilated in slow-motion or better yet by a series of shots of the principal peak moments of the action, shown at greater length. Here again the simplicity and economy of slides can often outweigh their lack of movement. And, while on the subject of crafts, let us not overlook the point that most pupils very naturally keep the paintings, sculpture, ceramics or other objects that they have made, and that a colour reproduction of the most notable of these items is of value for the school archives, both as a record and as a guide for future students.

These are the principal stages in a visual aid to the making of sculptures in plaster on a metal armature. The complete presentation consisted of about 20 slides. Such a subject may well be photographed in colour reversal on 35mm film as a basis for a slide-tape feature, and with another camera (if possible on a larger size such as 6 × 6 cms) on black-and-white negative for enlargement as a wall chart. The version projected in colour with a soundtrack will have a more immediate appeal and may decide the student to attempt this type of work for himself; the monochrome wall chart will serve as a reminder when he is actually trying his hand at it.

INDOOR SHOOTING WITH FLASH

Even when photographed in the daytime, most general views of schoolrooms have to be assisted by electronic flash or blue flash-bulbs, in view of the enormous contrast between the indoor and the outdoor lighting, particularly when a window is included in the shot. When using this combination the important point to remember is that the choice of shutter speed does not affect the exposure of the flash. The discharge of an electronic flash has a duration of around 1/800 sec. Consequently the shutter speed cannot influence the intensity of the beam, but only the amount of daylight that reaches the film.

The normal procedure is to determine the exposure required for the outside daylight, and set the shutter and lens opening accordingly; then to divide the guide number of the flash by the *f*/stop already chosen. The resulting number is the distance from the subject at which the flash should be placed in order to illuminate it with a brilliance equal to that of daylight. As this looks rather artificial, it is preferable for the flash to be about 50 per cent further away, giving a contrast range of 2:1.

Be careful not to take such a picture when facing a window, as the light from the flashgun will be reflected in the glass.

BOUNCE FLASH AND EXTENSION HEADS

There are different solutions to the problem of taking pictures indoors after sunset. The main difficulty when using flash as the only source of light is that the intensity of the beam falls off very rapidly. In a general interior view, if you expose for the foreground, the back of the room looks almost black; if the lens is opened up to cover the maximum distance, the nearest subjects are completely 'washed out'. One way to overcome this, if the room has a white ceiling and light-coloured walls, is to point the reflector upwards so that the centre of the beam strikes the ceiling. This reflects the light on to the background, and only the edge of the beam illuminates the foreground directly. In this case the lens must be opened by one or two stops. If the flashgun is sufficiently powerful, it can be directed completely away towards the ceiling and wall *behind* the camera, and bounced back from these reflecting surfaces towards the subject. This gives an evenly diffused light very suitable for colour, but the ceiling and walls must of course be white or of a very pale hue, otherwise the picture will have a colour cast. As a lot of light is lost by this system, the aperture has to be increased by at least two or even three stops.

An extension head (a second flashhead on a long lead set off simultaneously with the first on the camera) can bring a great improvement to the rendering. Its only inconvenience is that in many situations an assistant is needed to hold it, but in the school photography we are discussing this is easy enough to find. In a general view of an empty room, he would stand to the side (out of the field of the camera!) about half way down, pointing the auxiliary unit towards the back wall. In a schoolroom filled with seated students, the assistant could stand on a chair, holding the unit at arm's length pointed down at an angle of 45°.

When photographing individual subjects, the extension head may be used as the main modelling light, the lamp on the camera being considered as a fill-in to lighten the shadows. Its intensity can be controlled to a certain extent by covering it with one or more layers of white gauze, which also help to soften the harsh effect of direct flash. (Note: I am referring to electronic flash; a flashbulb becomes very hot, and gauze might be burned if placed close to it.)

SHOOTING POTTERY AND SCULPTURE

Soft lighting is not suitable for all subjects; pottery and in particular sculpture may be more strikingly interpreted by means of strong contrasts that bring out the form and modelling. Generally the main light is placed at 45° above and to the side, but the illumination must be modified according to the subject. If the sculpture is an interpretation of the human body, or a bust, then the criteria of portrait photography can be applied, particular care being taken to avoid deep shadows in the eye sockets, crossed lights that form double shadows, or excessive backlighting. But in the more likely event of the sculpture being an abstract design, illumination should be of the type used for still life – perhaps with oblique lighting to accentuate the texture of the stone or wood.

Normal or even long-focus lenses are to be preferred, because a very close viewpoint creates distortion; and unless an effect of foreshortening is desired, the viewpoint should be straight on to the centre. This is especially important with ceramics: round dishes photographed at an angle appear oval and tall pots become squat. As a general rule, backgrounds should be plain, unobtrusive and of neutral colour, but wood or rough-textured fabric such as jute make a pleasing contrast with smooth glazed pottery.

Making Slide-tape Work for You

Good relations with customers are all-important in business, and one of the principal ways of maintaining them is to keep present and future clients informed of the firm's activities. Big companies are well aware of this, and each week dozens of 16mm documentary, factual and industrial films are released, dealing with industry, medicine, travel, social questions – in fact every imaginable subject from agriculture to zoology. These films are often admirably presented and interesting even to the layman, but one snag is inherent to them all: they are costly, and therefore only major corporations, or public services, can afford to produce them.

Yet even more than large firms, small businesses need to get across to prospective clients exactly what they can offer, and many have failed because they were unable to do so although their work was of a high standard. If you are selling toothpaste, you can take a tube around with you; if you are a printer or an artist you can show samples of your skill; but suppose that you manufacture large and cumbersome equipment or provide certain services, how do you make the point? A brochure or leaflet *describes* but does not *show*, and is not very exhilarating in this audio-visual age. Far better to present a well-produced series of slides with an accurate and lively soundtrack; the impact can be remarkable. Yet you can make it yourself, at very little expense.

Government departments make productions for nation-wide distribution, but many municipalities need documents of a local nature. How many old houses, pulled down to make way for new building sites, have disappeared without trace, because although interesting they were not of sufficient architectural or historic importance to be included in the National Building Record? How many voices or sounds will never be heard again, because no one thought to tape them before it was too late?

PORTRAIT OF A NEIGHBOURHOOD

As examples, let us imagine various slide-tape features produced in the same small town. They make use of many similar slides, but are oriented for different purposes, either documentary or commercial.

The first, based on the history and development of the locality in general, is made for the municipal archives. Just because it is an official record, it need not be dry as dust and boring. Many great photographers and film-makers have been inspired to memorable work by the everyday activities of a town. Berenice Abbott, whose celebrated photographic series *Changing New York* – made for the Works Progress Administration – is now exhibited in that city's museum, wrote that 'making the portrait of a town is the work of a lifetime, and one portrait is not enough, as it changes so fast. Everything in a town tells its life-story: its great body of stone, brick, wood, steel and glass, the breathing of its men and women, its roads stretching to infinity – the life-force flowing in its veins . . .'.

In 1927, Walter Ruttmann's film *Berlin, Symphony of a City* created a style which has often been copied. Ruttmann decided that he would do without actors or even a story-line, and that the hero of his film would be the city itself. The separate images were linked together by visual resemblance: a symphony orchestra to instruments in a music-hall band, the legs of the chorus to the legs of participants in a bicycle race. The basic idea is still valid today, although it need not be carried to such lengths.

Other slide-tape features made in the town would not attempt to give an overall impression of it, but could concentrate on certain of its aspects: civic projects, cultural activities such as art festivals, industrial development, recreational facilities or educational advancement. As well as building up archives, they would assist the community by helping in the study of present situations and the planning of future action.

DISSEMINATING BUSINESS INFORMATION

Audio-visual presentations have many uses in business, but especially in the form of publicity (letting the public know what a firm is doing) and advertising (transforming that public into prospective buyers). More concisely, these two principles could be called *telling* and *selling*. Telling does not exclude the eventual possibility of selling, of course, but it is more vague and subtle, and presented in the form of information.

Perhaps an estate agent might make a slide-tape feature in order to take his clients on conducted tours of the town without leaving his office; he would naturally concentrate on the practical aspects: shopping centre, public services, entertainments – but he should not overlook some pleasant views of the park or surrounding countryside.

Or what could be more interesting to the prospective customers of a building contractor than actually to see the progression of a site from the clearing of the ground to the completion of the estate? And a certain lyricism could be mixed in with business in a slide-tape production made by a landscape designer, illustrating, with musical accompaniment, the various changes wrought by the seasons in his gardens. . . .

It is good business sense for a firm to keep the public informed of its activities, but it is its duty to reveal them to its shareholders.

Photojournalism is much used nowadays in the preparation of annual reports, to give a review of corporate operations as a whole and an accounting of the company's progress. This printed documentation is made attractive and readable by placing the required financial information among a series of photographs that subtly portray the desired image of the firm.

At an annual general meeting, both the image and the information can be presented in an even more interesting manner by projecting the photographs on a screen and accompanying them by a soundtrack. In most cases, the producer of such a slide-tape feature will find that its preparation is not necessarily arid; it can allow him as much freedom and imagination as a magazine assignment, and he may even discover himself to be a part of a creative team, contributing his own ideas and concepts as well as pictures and sound recordings. But he must never forget that he is dealing with facts; and while presenting them as eloquently and artistically as he can, he must bear in mind that his purpose is not essentially art, but *communication*.

High-pressure salesmanship, in which the poor client's resistance was battered down by an overpowering flow of talk, has fortunately been abandoned by most firms and replaced by the well-schooled manner, based on a study of his likes, dislikes and reasons for buying a product. In the jargon beloved of experts, this is called 'customer motivation', a phrase which covers everything from a desire for increased social status to relief from worry, from sheer physical pleasure to simple convenience.

Even man's love of others – notably of his family – is studied, because this is the major *motivation* for purchases made for children. Consequently the most successful advertisements are those that prove to the prospective buyer that the product can satisfy a basic want. But they must be convincing: people will not buy a product if they do not believe what is said about it.

The devices that convince are simple: realistic photographs, 'before and after' pictures, testimonials, visual demonstrations – and a pleasing and friendly voice.

As to the equipment required for the photography and recording of this type of production (whether its purpose is documentary, or for publicity or advertising) it can often be very simple too, although certain large gatherings may require more material and skill.

AIDS TO SAFETY PRECAUTIONS

According to a survey published in the *Reader's Digest* (September 1970), in one year a million Britons are victims of on-the-job accidents serious enough to keep them out of work for at least three days, several hundred are permanently incapacitated and more than a thousand killed. 'No amount of legislating can eliminate accidents caused by disregard for personal safety,' it says. 'Safety experts in government and industry agree that education in safety for all workers is a matter of top priority if the toll of on-the-job accidents is to be reduced . . . what is required is safety consciousness and safety training in every place of work in Britain.'

Many first-rate visual-aids and films exist, notably those produced by the Royal Society for the Prevention of Accidents, but here again, as in the case of training aids in schools, they are necessarily of a generalized nature. Even though it be less skilfully presented than a professional feature, a production made on the spot, dealing with specific events and local people known to the audience, is bound to have more impact and be longer remembered – and so will fulfil its purpose better.

ESSENTIAL QUALITIES OF INFORMATIVE FEATURES

Whether produced for telling or selling, no feature can succeed unless it is clear, accurate and pleasing.

Clarity is essential both in the picture and the commentary, but especially for the latter, which must be adapted to the powers of understanding of an average public. Technical terms should be used very rarely, and only after their meaning has been explained. On the other hand, the desire to simplify or to render certain points more intelligible must not lead to approximations of the truth. A specialist of the subject being described should be able to see the feature without being irritated by inaccuracies. The third quality applies to most types of production. The presentation should be attractive, even if it cannot be entertaining. The ideal is to be both, with a touch of humour as well, if possible.

All this is really common sense: if the spectator is bored, or cannot understand what is being explained to him, the feature is a waste of time and has not succeeded in its purpose.

EQUIPMENT FOR MAKING FEATURES

Many of the photographs have to be taken rapidly, when the occasion presents itself, so the equipment should be compact and portable. A simple easy-load push-button type of camera is the most suitable, although a more bulky single-lens reflex may be necessary for some shots such as close-ups or reproductions of charts and graphs. These are best taken when plenty of time is available for setting up a tripod and arranging the background and lighting.

Cassette recorders are useful for carrying around when gathering information or taking photographs. They give quite reasonable results and are easy to handle. The tiny incorporated loudspeaker cannot be expected to provide high-fidelity sound, however, and it is advisable to re-record the tape on to spools later.

When considerable sound material is needed, such as a record of a meeting, a banquet or perhaps a wedding, you will be faced with some of the most complex problems that can beset an amateur recordist. An acceptable, coherent recording of the multitude of sounds made by a number of people in a large room, hall or church cannot be obtained without advance preparation and a wide assortment of equipment.

Just as multiple lighting is usually necessary to take photographs of such scenes, so it cannot be expected that a single microphone will be able to cover them. When attending a business or social function, we listen selectively and our brain decides which information is important and which is not, sorting it out from the mass of noise carried to it by the ear. But even the most sophisticated modern microphone does not have a brain; it cannot unravel one sound from another.

Therefore you may need three or more microphones, placed in strategic positions, linked to a mixer with sufficient inputs under the control of a recordist who will fade each up or down according to the situation.

At an annual general meeting or a dinner, the speeches come mainly from a central point at a top table, but you should try to find out beforehand whether questions or proposals are likely to come from different parts of the room. It may be possible to record all the principal declarations on two microphones located close together at the top table, in which case their audio leads can be paralleled to arrive at a common recorder input. Better results are likely with additional microphones in the body of the room, because not only will interventions from other speakers be heard clearly, but an atmosphere of listener-reaction will be recorded along with the main speeches. But the 'recording engineer' must be careful to dose this lightly so as not to swamp out what is being said.

A church wedding adds the possibility of a hollow, echoing effect to the other complications. Three microphones are really essential, and of course it is only courteous to visit the officiating clergyman before the ceremony to obtain his permission to install them and perhaps make some preliminary tests. One microphone should be placed near the bride and groom to record the vows, another near the altar for the prayers and address, and the third arranged for the best recording of general hymn singing by the congregation (but don't put it near the organ!).

PROJECTION TO THE CLIENT

It is of course preferable for commercial slide-sound productions to be pre-synchronized by means of recorded pulses. For an individual showing before just one or two clients, a new type of equipment is now appearing on the market in the form of a compact valise containing an automatic projector linked to a cassette recorder and incorporating a small back-projection screen. For projection, the slide-magazine is attached to the projector, the appropriate cassette inserted and the show goes on by itself. It is not even necessary to darken the room.

For shows by front projection before a slightly larger audience, in rooms that are difficult to black out, 'daylight' screens exist, one particularly brilliant example being the *Ektalite* manufactured by Kodak. This measures 40 × 40 in. and performs remarkably: a slide can actually be viewed on it in the open, although it is intended for semi-darkened interiors. There is only a little fall-off at the sides, but a certain amount in the vertical plane, so positioning is important.

Three snags that must be mentioned are that the screen is rigid – it cannot be folded at all – which makes it difficult to carry about despite its relatively small size; its surface is very delicate and should be protected when not in use; and perhaps most important it is expensive.

Dual Projection Methods

We have discovered how to make the best use of our slides, how to record a soundtrack that is pleasing, instructive or evocative (with luck, all three at once), and the way to put them together to produce a presentation known as a slide-tape feature. We can now step forward to the ultimate stage in amateur slide-tape production – to what I do not hesitate to describe as one of the most exciting developments in showmanship ever devised. A word of warning, however. This method offers such possibilities that once you have seen it you may wish that your slides should never be presented in any other way. And that is indeed how it should be approached – by seeing it in action, for no words can really explain the effect it produces on the spectator.

Like most good ideas, the system is basically simple. It employs dual projection, that is to say two projectors instead of the usual one. Placed side by side, or one above the other, they fill the screen in exactly the same manner, and make use of the same set of slides, which is divided between them. This is not as extravagant as it appears, because the results are far more interesting than before.

BRIDGING THE GAP

In a normal slide show, the most irritating thing is the blackout between each image, which not only breaks the spell but causes visual fatigue. The obvious way to eliminate that gap is to place another picture in it by means of a second identical projector. If a variable diaphragm or some other form of mask is mounted in front of the lens of each machine and the two are linked together, so that one opens as the other closes, the screen is continuously illuminated. By placing slides Nos. 1,3,5,7 etc. in one projector and Nos. 2,4,6,8 etc. in the other, they can be shown without a break.

This is already a satisfactory result though not, in fact, very original: magic lanterns linked in pairs were operating in the nineteenth century under the name of Dissolving Views. They were an early ancestor of the cinema. In those days the manipulation was difficult; today the mechanism is a pleasure to use.

The black hole has disappeared; but simultaneously, as unexpected free gifts, appear two important possibilities that transform slide presentation even further. We can now add the dynamic technique of rhythm to the passage of the images, and we can conjure up certain fascinating visual effects.

ADDING RHYTHM AND EFFECTS

If the change-over from one projector to the other is made abruptly, the succession of the slides is instantaneous. In the language of cinema, this is known as a 'cut'. But if the diaphragms are manoeuvred slowly, one fades out as the other fades in: the result on the screen is a mix or dissolve. If one image is replaced by a completely black frame, the previous picture gradually darkens to a fade-out. Therefore the shots can now appear and even re-appear in time to music, cutting briskly on rhythmic beats, melting slowly in a more romantic mood.

As the slides mix into one another, a third image is seen between them, which if carefully planned can be a picture in its own right. For instance: in a Spring sequence, we have a view of the village church seen at a distance. The next shot is a close-up of blossom on a branch. If the two shots are composed correctly, during the dissolve the church spire appears framed by the blossom. Simple blending such as this can be very pleasing but it must not be overdone. Such effects are not an end in themselves, but are to be used at certain peak moments to lend extra interest.

DUAL-PROJECTION APPARATUS

Basically, the method requires two identical projection systems and a device enabling them to be alternately (and progressively) blacked-out. There are various ways of obtaining this result, and they also go in pairs.

ELECTRIC OR MECHANICAL

Fading may be electric (by dimming the lamps) or mechanical (by placing some sort of mask before the lenses). Electric fading has its devotees as it is economical and easy to set up; but it cannot give the very rapid change-over possible with masks, and there is a risk of colour-change when the lamps are dimmed.

DIAPHRAGM OR SHUTTER

If mechanical, the mask can consist of iris diaphragms – large versions of the one in a camera, that open and shut with a circular movement – or it can be made from metal 'shutters' with circular openings that slide across each other. Iris diaphragms are fairly expensive; they give excellent results on condition that they are mounted very close to the lens, otherwise the fade-out becomes an 'irising-out' from the edges towards the centre of the image.

The earliest masking system is a simple wiping device which is mentioned in very early descriptions of magic lanterns. The serrated edges helped to produce a smoother transition. An improved and efficient version of this primitive design is available commercially.

Many keen amateurs have made their own change-over units. The method often employed is that of the double sliding shutter, consisting of a metal frame with a pair of grooves in which two masks slide back and forth. The masks are best made of metal but

A simple mechanical wiping device used with magic lanterns. The transition was made a little smoother by the serrated edges.

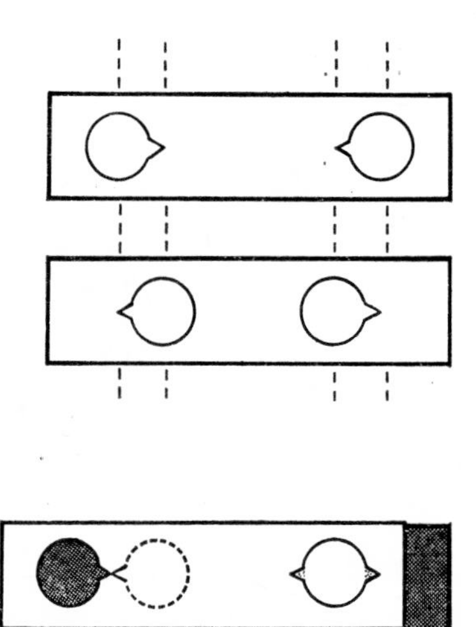

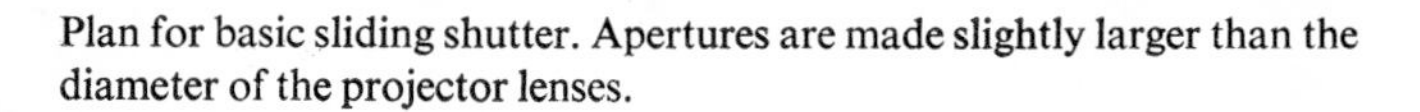

Plan for basic sliding shutter. Apertures are made slightly larger than the diameter of the projector lenses.

can even be of cardboard if they are not to be extensively used. An operating lever is attached to thin cables running over pulleys to pull them in opposite directions simultaneously by the method employed for curtains. The apertures are not entirely circular, but have a pointed notch at the side. The notches face each other on one shutter and are on the outside rim of the other. Without these notches, the dissolve would not be even, but resemble a crescent-shaped double wipe.

SEPARATE OR ALL-IN-ONE

The equipment may be devised from two similar projectors, but some firms are now manufacturing special machines that incorporate a dual mechanism in one unit. The most economical way to start experimenting is with two inexpensive projectors and a home-made masking device; and if you already own a good automatic machine you will probably wish to keep it and make use of a second one of the same type. But there is much to be said in favour of the special dual-projector, especially for portability and ease of setting up.

VERTICAL OR HORIZONTAL

If two separate single projectors are used, they may be placed side by side or mounted vertically one above the other. In the latter case a special support must be constructed. This arrangement is compact and may be set on a normal projection stand, but it cannot be used with the system of sliding shutters, as the frame holding them extends beyond the projectors. Used vertically it might need counterweights to prevent the shutters from slipping out of place.

EARLY PRESENTATION METHODS

The earliest public audio-visual presentations combining the projection of images with a sound accompaniment were given in Paris with great success at the time of the French Revolution. They were created by a mysterious personnage who called himself Robertson, although that was probably not his real name. He also invented names for his spectacle and for the apparatus that enabled him to produce it. The shows were known as Phantasmagories, a word that has remained in the language, and the magic-lantern on wheels, which could move silently around on rails, was called a Fantascope.

Apart from being an excellent physicist and illusionist, Robertson was a remarkable showman. He installed himself near the Place Vendôme in the old buildings of a convent closed down by the revolutionaries. His auditorium was the chapel. The spectators had to pass through the ruined cloister and along creepy corridors before finding themselves before a door covered in hieroglyphs that opened on to a gloomy room lined with black curtains and feebly illuminated by 'a sepulchral lamp'. Robertson then appeared, and conjured up the phantoms. The apparitions were accompanied by noises of thunder, funeral bells and rain. Spots of light grew larger and larger, transforming themselves into huge ghosts that seemed to jump at the audience before vanishing.

A few years later, after Bonaparte came to power, Robertson added political propaganda to his productions. In his Memoirs he quotes this description printed in the journal *Courrier des Spectacles* in November 1800: 'Robespierre emerges from his tomb and tries to rise, but lightning reduces the monster to powder. . . . Diogenes, holding his lantern, is looking for a man and in so doing seems to pass through the audience . . . a brilliant star shines out of the chaos, the clouds disperse to reveal the visage of Bonaparte. Minerva

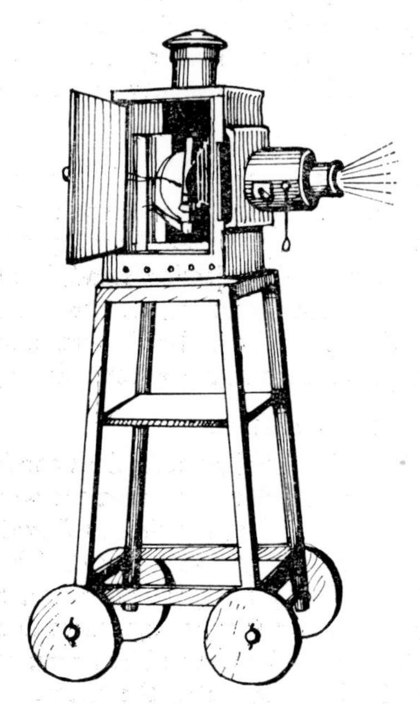

Robertson's 'Fantascope'.

places a crown of olive branches on the brow of the young hero. . . . Needless to say, this ingenious allegory is always greeted with enthusiasm.'

Equally ingenious was the mechanism which kept the image in focus while the lantern was wheeled to and from the back-projection screen. Robertson also made use of small secondary projectors operated by assistants who sometimes had them strapped to their chests as they moved about.

But it was in England that slide shows really came into their own, and by the second half of the nineteenth century many halls were presenting continuous programmes of Dissolving Views obtained by means of dual projection. The repertoire was varied. As might be expected in Victorian days, there was an abundance of educational and uplifting subjects, but entertainment was represented also, by adaptations of nursery rhymes, Robinson Crusoe, Walter Scott and even Shakespeare. Excerpts from these books or plays were read aloud as the slides were shown. In the United States, the vogue was for illustrated hymns, consisting of reproductions of instructional paintings projected in churches and mission halls while the congregation sang.

In 1870, Mr. Samuel Highley addressed the members of the (Royal) Photographic Society on the subject of 'The Magic Lantern in Relation to Photography'. He might have been speaking today. 'What can be more delightful', he asked, 'than to bring back reminiscences of travel, taken from our own points of view, and on one's return placing before family and friends enlarged transcripts, depicted by Old Sol, of the scenes that have given us health and pleasure? What can be more valuable for educational purposes than to place before the student or schoolboy accurate as well as striking pictures of the subjects of their studies, whether in science, geography or history, giving the next best thing to the students' having seen the objects themselves?'

TYPES OF LANTERN

Mr. Highley described various forms of lantern, explaining that for larger audiences the body of the lantern should be made 'of stout mahogany and the oldest material available, preferably old dining table tops'.

As we have noted, dual and even multiple projection already existed a century ago. Then, as now, the lanterns were placed either side by side or vertically.

The Dissolving-view Lantern was 'essentially arranged for the production of dioramic effects by the super-position of a painting placed in one stage over a scene projected from the other stage on to the screen'. One view gradually effaces another, or both are combined to produce effects such as 'a lightning flash over a stormy sea, fire and smoke rolling from a volcano or building, snow falling over a landscape, etc.'

If the electric light was replaced by gas, the Highly-Malden gas dissolver could be used. This was a multi-tap which transferred the gas supply from one projector to the other, giving the exhibitor greater command over the effects produced.

The triunial model, consisting of three vertically-mounted lanterns might have been intended for the presentation of colour-

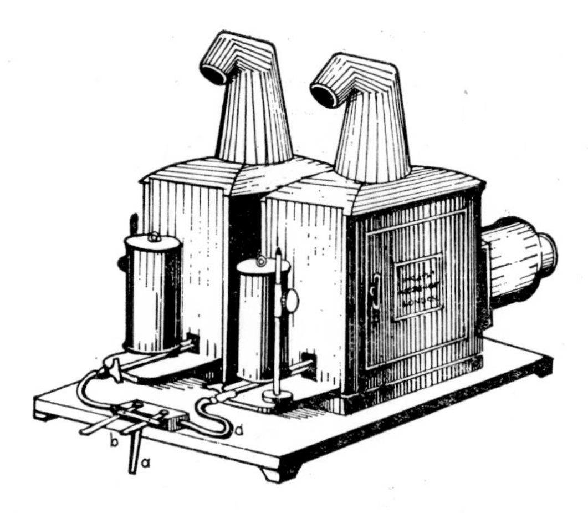

Dissolving-view lantern.

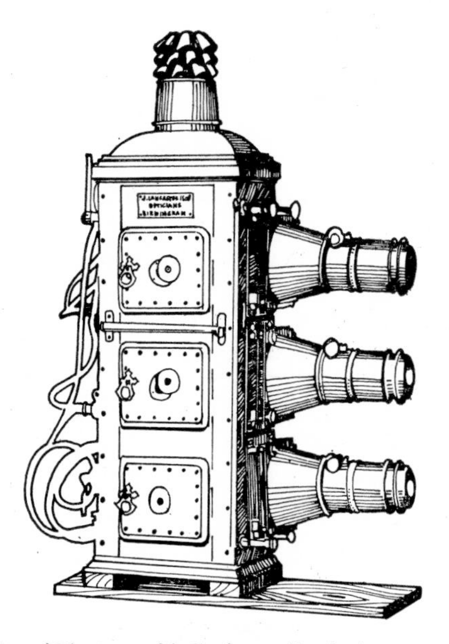

Triunial model (Royal Photographic Society collection).

Hughes Slide Holder.

Changeover unit, Paris, 1885.

separation positives, following the experiments by Maxwell and Ducos du Hauron of the additive colour process, in which three slides of the same subject taken through tricolour filters were superimposed by projection. But it is more likely that the machine was designed for dissolving views, the third picture allowing even more dramatic effects.

Other effects were produced by mechanized slide-holders incorporating levers and racks imparting a movement to silhouetted figures, as in the model designed in 1885 by a London optician named Hughes.

At about the same time, in Paris, a changeover unit was presented, with characteristics remarkably similar to those seen today.

ASSEMBLING AN ELECTRICAL DIMMING UNIT

The equipment required for dual projection is not necessarily complex, and it is possible for the handyman to assemble his own unit. The one illustrated below is the simplest of various models designed by Stanley W. Bowler. Intended to introduce the beginner to the possibilities of the system, it can be put together from standard apparatus and requires only a minimum of tools and woodworking skill.

The dissolve from one slide to the next is done electrically by dimming the lamp of one projector while that of the other increases

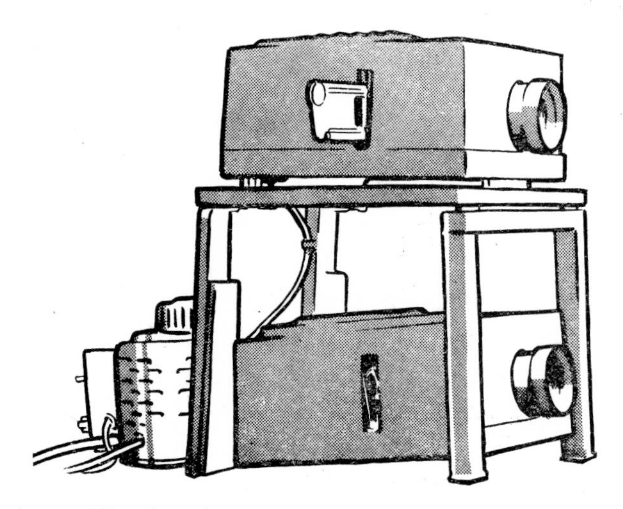

Simple electrical dimming unit.

in brilliance to its normal output. It must be admitted at once that this system has two disadvantages: the colour of the light from the lamp inevitably changes as the lamp is dimmed, becoming redder as the voltage drops; and a straightforward dissolve is the only possible effect that can be obtained, although the rate of dissolve is under the control of the projectionist. It is not possible, for instance, to bring back the preceding picture without dimming the second again. But a small advantage of electrical dimming over separate masks is the ease of lining-up the images on the screen. With mechanical systems, the projectors have to be lined up in relation to the masks or diaphragms as well as to each other.

The electrical control used is a special kind of transformer wound on a tubular core, over the windings of which passes a spring-loaded carbon-brush contact. It should be capable of carrying a current of 1–2 amps, depending on the current consumption of the projector lamps and fans, if used.

The projectors are fitted with quite heavy three-core flexible leads (which were shortened back to suit) properly colour-coded so that each of the items on the baseboard is earthed, via the green core, and the earth continuity is carried right back to the main 13 amp 3-pin fused plug (fitted with a 2-amp fuse for complete protection).

A brief description of the stand is of interest, as it can be used as a basis for a different assembly with other projectors. As dimensions vary from one type to another, no detailed dimensions are given.

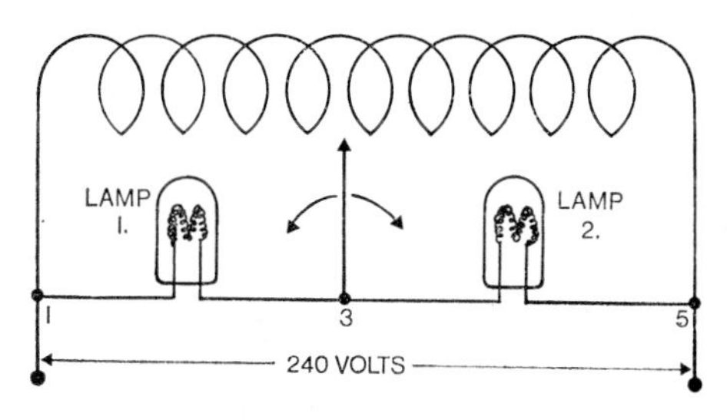

Dual projector electrical control.

The baseboards for the lower and upper projectors are cut from $\frac{3}{8}$ in. thickness multi-ply wood, the lower being about 12 × 18 in. overall and the upper about 9 × 10 in. – just sufficient to provide a platform with the minimum of border. The centre line of the machines is off-set to the left-hand side of the main base so that when the slide carriers are pulled out they do not overhang and there is space for racking the slides to be shown. The transformer control is mounted at the rear of the board, with a pair of similar 2 amp 3-pin sockets fixed to left and right of it. (These *non-preferred* standard sockets were chosen to prevent any other electrical equipment being plugged into the outlets of this assembly.)

A front slot (4 × $\frac{5}{8}$ in.) and a pair of holes ($\frac{5}{8}$ in. dia.) were cut right through the $\frac{3}{8}$ in. multi-ply. Slips of $\frac{1}{8}$ in. ply were then glued and pinned on the underside of the baseboard to make recesses into which the feet of the projector then fitted. These hold the projectors quite securely.

Next, if the projectors are not fitted with blower cooling it is essential to ensure that there is a free flow of air under them. For this reason, two large cut-outs (each 4 × 5 in.) were made in the appropriate places. Then, in order to ensure that the lower one is fully effective, $\frac{1}{2}$ in. high rubber feet were fitted to the four corners of the main baseboard. Incidentally, the electrical control system used for this method of dissolving view projection has just one more practical attribute, and that is that only one lamp is alight at any time, reducing the problem of over-heating by half.

Over the front end of the lower machine is a simple 'bridge' consisting of two uprights of 1-in. dia. dowel (broomstick will serve) with a cross-bar joining their tops. Behind the lower unit there is a pair of similar hinged struts which consist of two sliding pieces of stripwood, one carrying a threaded screw and wingnut and the other a slot in which the screw slides. This arrangement allows the rear end of the upper platform to be raised to bring the optical axes of the two projectors into line on the screen. Even if not set up precisely, the normal levelling front foot of the machine can still be used for final trimming.

The front end of the upper platform has a central fixing only – between the underside and the cross-bar there is a small spacer through which a single wood-screw passes. On the upper side is a small compression spring to hold the platform in position and yet allow it to be tilted laterally, by adjusting one or other of the two slidable legs differently, should it be necessary for this to be done.

Finally, the platforms were given several thin coats of sealer to protect the wood and to make cleaning simple The cut edges of the plywood were trimmed with extruded plastic hockey-stick-section moulding, which also provides a lip to prevent odd items from rolling off the baseboard.

All of the parts mentioned may be obtained from any well-stocked do-it-yourself establishment, the electrical components are standard items sold even in chain stores and the whole assembly should not take the average handy-man more than a few hours to make.

VERTICAL SYSTEM WITH IRIS DIAPHRAGMS

This unit, which is now showing signs of wear, is included here not only because of its functional design but for sentimental reasons; it was with this set-up that I presented in public my very first Diaporama *La Dame Blanche*, an evocation of the youth of Mary, Queen of Scots, that included the slow dissolve from engravings of a public execution to a scarlet rose-bush which has become well known since, having been mentioned in various articles on dual-projection. After nearly ten years of being transported around from one show to another, the device is in good working order and I still use it for occasional presentations.

It was designed and made by Paul Napoleoni, of Fontainebleau, France and consists of a pair of manually operated semi-automatic projectors, mounted vertically on a metal stand. On the front part of this are fixed two iris-diaphragms linked together by rods centered on a cog-wheel. Movement of the manipulating handle is transmitted to the cog by means of gearing to slow down the motion, but a very brisk cut is also possible by pulling the lever smartly. The top platform, to which the upper projector is attached from below, can be

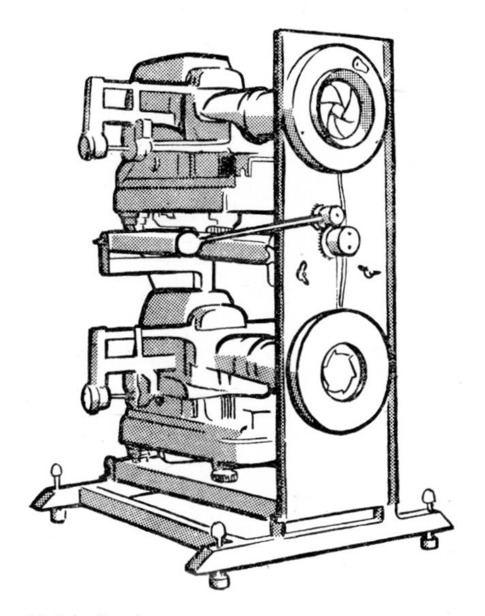

Vertical system with iris diaphragms.

adjusted for superimposition of the images by wing-nuts at its corners.

To change the slides, the projector knob is pulled out, given a quarter turn and pushed in again. Doing this on two machines alternately, while manoeuvring the dissolve handle at various speeds in sync with the track, might seem to require the talents of a conjurer, but in fact after a little rehearsal the whole operation is quite simple. Indeed the main advantage of manual slide-changing is its rapidity – with practice one can do it more quickly than an automatic machine, as I discovered to my dismay when attempting to project at a photo club a fast-moving sequence I had often shown with ease on this unit. The club's equipment consisted of two excellent fully-automatic projectors whose only defect was that the mechanism worked with ponderous majesty. By the time they had condescended to replace one slide by another, its allotted span was already passed. After half-a-dozen such movements I was so behind the soundtrack that it was impossible to catch up with it again, and the presentation had to stop. Fortunately I had brought my own equipment with me in case of emergency and was able to set it up and project the feature at the intended speed.

As in the electric-dissolve unit devised by Mr. Bowler, placing the projectors one over the other is essential in this case because the

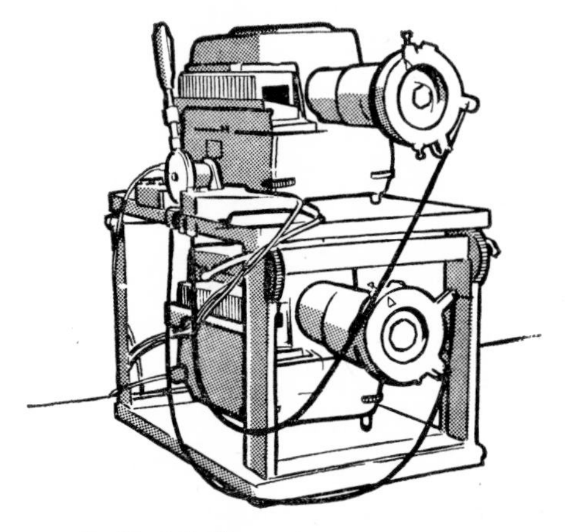

Automatic change vertical installation.

slide-changing lever is on their right, and if the machines were side by side, the lever of the left-hand one would be between the two, and so impossible to manipulate unless they were very far apart. Here all the controls are close together.

The main disadvantage of this vertical assembly is that it is rather less stable than a horizontal arrangement and needs a firm support if it is not to tremble during the constant manual operations.

AUTOMATIC-CHANGE VERTICAL INSTALLATION

An apparatus designed and put together by the members of the *Club des Amateurs Photographes de Champagne-sur-Seine* is based on two identical fully automatic projectors and two iris-diaphragms specially devised to fit directly around the front of projection lenses and fixed to them by means of tightening screws. The irises are operated by cables connected to a swivelling handle which, as it is pushed from one side to the other on its axis, opens one diaphragm and closes the other.

This equipment was used for several years to present the public performances of the entries in the Vichy slide-tape Festival. It has now been replaced by electrically controlled semi-automatic apparatus. The manually-operated projectors were placed side by side at the back of the theatre stalls. Fitted with 200mm lenses, they filled a screen approximately four metres wide. The changeover unit, also manually operated, was made by members of the club to a design based on the sliding shutter system described on page 116. Two operators fed the slides into the projectors, while a third was in charge of the manipulation of the dissolve lever, following instructions either given in an accompanying booklet or recorded on the lower track of the tape.

The handle is clamped to the side of the top platform of the stand, and the two remote slide-changing push-buttons of the projectors fixed on each side of it in such a way that the handle depresses the button as it arrives at the end of its course. A little spring rejects the handle so that it is not held down permanently on the button, as this would make the projector mechanism change several slides in succession.

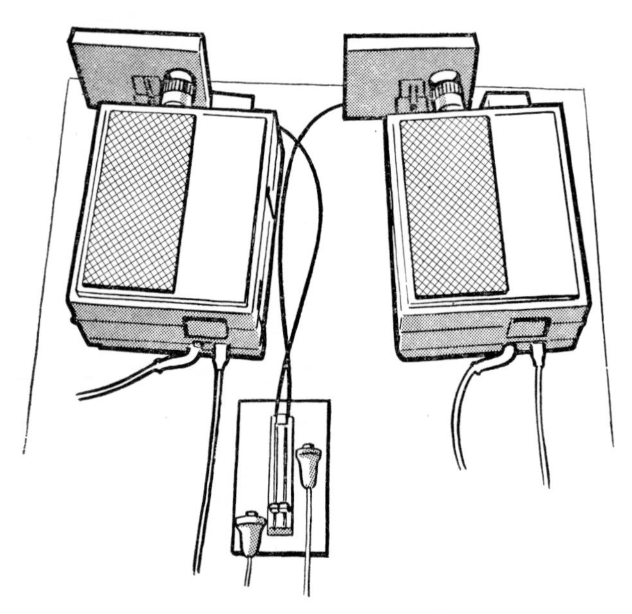

'Purlock Duo-Fade' in position in front of two projectors. This commercially-available dissolving device differs from the previously described models in that each shutter is independent. For normal changeover the cables are operated together, but for special effects it is possible to keep one shutter open while manipulating the other. The classic example of this technique is a series of main titles, in which a background image remains on the screen while slides bearing the lettering (in white on a black ground) are succesively faded in and out over it.

There is only one small defect in this otherwise excellent system. In order to work smoothly, the cable linking the handle to the iris diaphragms must be carefully positioned and, as the diaphragms are screwed to the front of the lens, any adjustment of the focusing during projection can only be very slight. To make major adjustments it is necessary to loosen the fixing screws and hold the diaphragm in place while turning the lens in its mount.

Special Effects

One of the most common effects used during projection is the dissolve. Some types of apparatus are equipped with a mechanism that produces dissolves automatically (in certain cases at three speeds, arbitrarily called fast, normal and slow). This may be of use when the presentation is to be entirely electronic, but for a personal show no machine can replace the subtle touch that the producer can bring by manipulation of the change-over lever. In order to make clear the possibilities of this technique, let us review the effects obtainable, with examples of each.

NORMAL-SPEED DISSOLVE

The control lever is pushed smoothly and continuously from one extremity to the other, the total passage lasting about 2 sec. This is the basic change-over, used when there is no rhythmic or visual reason to employ another form of transition.

RAPID CUTS

The lever is swept across to produce an instantaneous switch from one slide to the next. The movement should be swift but not brutal, and requires a little practice to bring it gently to a stop without banging the slide-change micro-switch, which may be delicate.

SLOW DISSOLVE

To obtain a slow dissolve, the movement must begin very gently, because some masks or diaphragms open abruptly and the second image is seen too soon in its entirety. When diaphragms are used, the only solution is to practise until a barely perceptible movement can be achieved at the start, becoming slightly faster and then slowing down again at the end. When the change-over takes place by a system of sliding shutters, their apertures must be carefully studied to ensure that the angle of the notch is sufficiently narrow. It is this notch or slot in the side of the opening that produces a smooth dissolve; without it the two circular holes would produce the effect of a sideways wipe.

MEDIUM-SPEED DISSOLVE WITH PAUSE IN THE MIDDLE

Where two pictures have been planned to 'go together', this can be marked by stopping the change-over halfway when both are seen, and holding the effect for 3 or 4 sec before continuing the movement of the dissolve.

FLICKERING EFFECTS AND RHYTHM

When the control lever is in the midway position, it can be jiggled back and forth rapidly to give an impression of scintillations. This effect is only useful for certain subjects and should not be used often as it soon becomes tiring to watch.

The illustrations are a sequence from a feature called *A Man and his Dream,* and show the result of a challenge to produce by the

Visual comparison of the shape of a church spire and the attitude of prayer. When the two shots are on the screen at once, the spire is superimposed over the triangular formation of the hands.

simple means of slide-tape a sequence that would seem to be reserved strictly for cinema: an automobile accident. The sound-track plays an important role, of course, and consists of a commercial recording of a car crash – squealing tyres and brakes, noise of tearing metal and falling glass.

The visuals consist of only these three images. The close-up of the man lighting his cigarette mixes in at normal speed as the music accompanying the previous sequence fades out. There is a short silence, then the sound of the crash begins. The shot of the car head-lamps cuts in rapidly and flickers in and out for some moments over the picture of the man, which abruptly disappears to be replaced by the third shot, an over-exposed blur of the man putting up his arm

'Flickering effects' sequence portraying the drama and confusion of a road accident.

to defend himself. The headlamp oscillations continue briefly over this image and then disappear as the noise of the accident ceases. A pause of a second or two, and then, as faint, calm music begins, the first shot of the next sequence mixes in very slowly.

Needless to say, some rehearsing is necessary before a combination of movements such as this can be presented in public. But once the mechanism is fully understood, it presents no real difficulty, and I would venture to say that it can be quite stimulating – rather like conducting an orchestra!

Photographically speaking, this sequence had to take place at night, because the car headlamps are in every sense the highlight of the effect. The first two pictures are straightforward time exposures taken outside, but the 'blur' photograph was in fact shot indoors against a dark background. The camera, on a tripod, was set on 1 sec, but also fitted with electronic flash. The man, lighted from the side by a floodlamp, made a fast gesture with his hand. The flash arrested part of the movement, but the time exposure blurred the rest. The overexposure is intentional, to give the impression of his being dazzled by the car lights.

RHYTHM

Instead of being jerked back and forth, the change-over lever can be pushed *forward* only, in short, sharp motions, preferably in time to music with a strong rhythmic beat. One slide-tape feature that has become a classic in its genre (*Jam-Color* by M. Bichet of France) relies entirely for its impact on a combination of flickering and rhythmic change-over, applied to close-ups of jazz musicians photographed during a jam session. This type of presentation is particularly disliked by purists of the cinema, who consider that it is an encroachment into their medium. We can ignore these woolly discussions, and make use of the effects in moderation when they are appropriate.

FORWARD AND BACKWARD MOVEMENT

This is a slow dissolve which goes only half-way, pauses a while and then *returns to the start* instead of continuing to the end of the movement. It is principally used for titles that are to be shown in cinematic fashion, appearing in white against a dark background. The presentation begins with the background slide, then the first title – in white lettering on a black ground – is projected over it. The two are held together for the time necessary to read the title, then that image is faded out by returning the lever to its original position and the second title-slide appears. When the title sequence is complete, the lever is pushed to the end of its course and the background slide is changed.

This effect changes the normal order of the transparencies and if the projectionist does not pay careful attention to what he is doing he can end up with the wrong slide – and once that has happened, the result is utter confusion. Furthermore the numbering of the pictures is affected and must be altered accordingly.

The opening sequence of my feature on the town of Fontainebleau is an example of this. The first six transparencies are as follows:

1. Eagle against blue sky.
2. Title 'Fontainebleau is my Town'.

3. MCU of gateway showing symbols 'N' and bees.
4. LS of courtyard.
5. Coloured woodcut of 'Napoleon's farewells'.
6. Palace staircase.

The normal arrangement of these transparencies in their two magazines ready for dual-projection with the odd numbers in one and the even numbers in the other would be:

First magazine
1. Eagle
3. Gateway.
5. Woodcut.
7. etc.

Second magazine
2. Title.
4. Courtyard.
6. Staircase.
8. etc.

But the order of projection will not be the usual 1 – 2 – 3 – 4 – 5 – 6; it has become 1 – 2 – 1 – 3 – 4 – 5 – 6. While the eagle is still on the screen, the title shot is replaced by the gateway, which must therefore be in the opposite magazine to the eagle. The loading of the boxes must be:

First magazine
1. Eagle.
4. Courtyard.
6. Staircase.
8. etc.

Second magazine
2. Title.
3. Gateway.
5. Woodcut.
7. etc.

The first magazine which started off with the odd-numbered slides suddenly holds the even numbers. This is not very important if it happens, as here, right at the beginning of the production; but should an effect of this type take place half-way through, the change of sequence can be disconcerting.

A simple solution is to give a half-number to the slide which

Combination of two slides with dark backgrounds to provide a third-image effect.

follows the one that has been shown twice. In this case, No. 3 becomes 2A and the final numbering arrangement is:

First magazine

1. Eagle.
3. Courtyard.
5. Staircase.
7. etc.

Second magazine

2. Title.
2A. Gateway.
4. Woodcut.
6. etc.

Dual projection allows lighter-toned images to be projected on to the black background to form a composite picture. The second, fourth and final shots are the result of the simultaneous projection of two slides composed to blend together.

DARK BACKGROUNDS

Dual projection resembles camera double exposure inasmuch as the most striking effects of superimposition require a black or at least very dark background. In daylight this can be achieved by a shaded area behind the main subject or in a part of the composition, but the best results are obtained when the lighting can be controlled indoors by artificial illumination. Outdoor night shots also provide jet-black backgrounds, as in the illustration of the final sequence of *Fontainebleau*. The eagle which introduced the production (then photographed in sunlight against a blue sky) now ends it as a night shot.

These images are presented by the 'medium-speed dissolve with a pause in the middle' method, plus a little flickering on the fireworks. Shot No. 3 is one of a series taken with the camera shutter open (see page 17). I must admit that at the time I considered it a failure in view of its lop-sided composition; but this was transformed into a distinct advantage when the other two slides were taken later to be shown with it.

FADE OUT

A gradually darkening screen is an elegant finish to a production, especially of a slow-moving and poetic type. It can be obtained by switching off the lamp of the projector not in use before beginning a final change-over; but this is one more thing to remember, and it is wiser to provide an opaque slide for the purpose by placing in a mount a piece of unexposed film or of thin black paper.

SLIDE PHOTOGRAPHY FOR DUAL PROJECTION

Once you are addicted to dual projection (and the habit becomes ingrained very rapidly) your entire conception of slide photography is modified. An attractively arranged, correctly exposed, beautifully coloured transparency no longer suffices, because you have to take into consideration three additional factors: format, possible trick effects, and something rather vague that could be called 'continuity-composition'.

FORMAT

If you use 126 or other sizes of film that give a square format, this does not apply to you. But if you are one of the many who take rectangular pictures on 35mm, you will have to decide whether you intend to go on holding your camera vertically for some shots or if you are prepared to use it only horizontally for your productions. A dissolve from an upright to a horizontal picture results in a cross-shape which distracts from the subject and also leaves parts of the screen unfilled. Nearly all producers of dual-projected features have abandoned vertical presentation. This adds a little difficulty to the photographing of certain subjects, but the problem is not insoluble and might even stimulate the imagination. If you develop a nostalgia for vertical shooting, you can always catch up between times by taking all your personal family transparencies that way.

TRICK EFFECTS 'IN CAMERA'

All the illustrations so far have been combinations of dissimilar photographs. It can be interesting to project successively two slides that are alike in all respects but one: for instance, the same framing, the same setting and the same lighting, but a person included in the first has moved, or disappeared altogether. A particularly attractive variation on this idea is a static scene in which the lighting changes.

For example, two slides of a statue are taken from an identical viewpoint, but in the first instance the lighting is on the left side, and in the second it is placed on the right. Presented by a slow dissolve, the impression given is that the illumination is moving around the statue. This is additionally intriguing if the colour of the light changes also by means of tinted gelatine in front of the lamp in one picture. The camera needs a very firm support because it must not move between shots and the slightest displacement caused by winding on the film can make a big difference in the framing.

The same technique can be used on a grander scale outdoors by natural lighting. A scenic view including a building whose outline is clearly defined against the sky is photographed in the daytime and again at sunset; on projection, night appears to fall (at the speed chosen by the projectionist) or if the slides are reversed, dawn will rise. If the camera cannot be left in place on its tripod for several hours, the position from which the first shot was taken must be carefully noted and the alignment of the scene checked in the viewfinder.

CONTINUITY-COMPOSITION

An effect of the above type can be considered as a trick, or more simply as an advanced example of 'continuity-composition'. When composing your picture you should try to bear in mind that it is not going to stand on its own merits alone, but will be part of a sequence. Whenever possible, the main subject should be presented in a way that will blend with the slides that are to precede and come after it. This can lead to an alteration in its position in the frame: a head-and-shoulders portrait will be composed more to one side in order to leave a space in which a full-length view of the figure is to appear – the latter also off-centered. Taken individually, the slides may seem unbalanced, but it is the result on projection that matters, and it will be more satisfying to see the side-by-side close-up and longshot of the person during changeover (a method often employed on TV) than for one to be superimposed, however briefly, on top of the other.

The reverse applies for the now-classic effect of a child's face appearing in the centre of a sunflower (the dark heart of the flower forming a perfect black spot for superimposition, the face standing out in sunlight against a shadowed background): a completely central composition being adopted here against all the rules of the 'golden mean'.

DOUBLE MOUNTING

The effects mentioned so far in this chapter are visible only on projection; they are the result of a blending of two slides which, when seen separately, do not appear any different from the normal, except perhaps from the point of view of their composition. But there are definite 'trick effects' that can be obtained either in the camera or when mounting the slide, and you might also like to make use of these occasionally.

One such effect is double mounting, already described in the paragraphs on titling. It consists of placing two slides together as a sandwich in the same glass mount. The important difference between double mounting and dual projection is that the technique of the latter is similar to classic double exposure in a cinecamera, which is to say that part of one image is blacked out to provide an unexposed (or in the case of projection, unlit) area for the second picture, either by covering it up or by arranging the lighting so that dark patches are left in both scenes. But if we were to use this procedure when double-*mounting*, the dark areas of the two images would obviously merely cancel each other out when placed one over the other, and we should find ourselves with a mainly black slide.

When sandwiching two transparencies together, certain parts of the picture must on the contrary be light in tone. In landscape shots this is relatively easy, and we have seen how a main title may be made by placing the lettering in a suitable sky area (see page 27). But there are multitudes of other possibilities: for example, portraits appearing through clouds, wintry trees in mist or ripples on water. Sometimes two overexposed slides, worthless when projected individually, can be saved by sandwiching them together – but such luck is not frequent and it is usually necessary to plan at least one of the two pictures.

DIFFUSION AND SOFT FOCUS

When a shot is taken slightly out of focus, details that should be represented by points are in fact rendered as minute circles which overlap and lend slight confusion to the outlines of the subject. Many early motion pictures made great use of this for sentimental close-ups where, with the additional assistance of a generous helping of back lighting, the heroine glowed in a nebulous aura that also helped to iron out any wrinkles (and at the same time, any personality). Considerable experimentation is necessary to discover by how much or how little the lens setting may be altered to give the desired result, for an acceptable soft focus soon becomes an irritating out of focus. So if you wish to apply some scatter to the highlights to give a dreamy or romantic effect, it is wiser to leave the focusing ring alone and to make use of diffusion.

The usual method is to place a small piece of glass in a frame a few inches before the lens, carefully shielded from direct light, and after cleaning both sides thoroughly, to take a trace of warm Vaseline on a finger-tip and rub it uniformly over the glass surface. If the grease is laid on with a circular motion, the diffusion will be radial. If it is applied horizontally, vertical diffusion results (i.e. the highlights will spread up and down) because the diffusion is always at right-angles to the direction of the smears. The whole subject need not be diffused; a clear space can be left for the principal figure. With a single-lens reflex camera, the effect obtained can be seen directly. Automatic diaphragms should be placed on 'manual' so that the result can be viewed at the shooting aperture, because the overall sharpness varies according to the lens opening.

If the plain glass is replaced by a piece of bottle glass such as a section broken from a jam jar, the scene becomes distorted in a nightmarish manner. The glass is turned about until the best angle is found and held in this position while the picture is taken (making sure that the hand holding it does not appear in the frame). The effect on exposure is negligible so long as the glass is clean and white, and even with tinted glass for coloured spectaculars, it is so slight that it can be ignored unless the hue is really deep.

DOUBLE EXPOSURE WITH GLASS

While on the subject of glass, I may as well mention its use in the making of double exposures, although the method is normally reserved for cinematographers filming ghostly apparitions, which in our case are more simply provided by the dual-projection system. Instead of mounting the pane of glass directly in front of the camera lens and photographing straight through it, you place it at an angle of 45° (as always, carefully shielded from direct light). A scene can then be viewed directly through the glass while at the same time another image – usually a single strongly lighted figure against a dark background – is reflected from a position at the side apparently over it. This optical illusion originated many years ago and used to provide a good deal of amusement in theatres, where it was called 'Pepper's Ghost' from the name of the gentleman who invented it. (On the stage it required a pane of glass as large as a shop window.)

NEED FOR MODERATION

All these effects, whether produced in the camera, or by superimposing slides in a mount, or during the presentation by manipulation of the changeover unit, add up to a formidable array of tricks at the disposal of a maker of slide-tape features. But their fascination must not lead him to concentrate on them too much, for his aim should always be to present an idea or story in as clear a manner as he can. This medium expresses itself by means of images and sounds, but in common with other languages it has punctuation and style. The variations in tempo brought by dissolves and cuts are its punctuation, and an occasional trick shot can add a lively touch of interest. But the basic language should be kept simple, and effects used with variety and moderation.

Clubs and Contests

Slide-tape features presented by dual projection originated in France, and spread with amazing rapidity throughout the country under the name of Diaporama. This name is coined from the word *diapositive* (a colour transparency) and the suffixe *orama* used currently for any spectacular show. The actual mechanical system of slide projection using two projectors is known as dual projection, but a new word was needed for the products shown by this method, which otherwise would have had to be called 'dual-projected slide-tape features'. A Diaporama still consists of a series of slides synchronized to a tape recording, but it has the particularity of being presented by dual projection. As a parallel, one could say that movie films are presented by means of cinematographic projection.

Few organizers of a competition or festival for slide-tape features would now consider showing them with a single projector; so as they are almost inevitably presented by dual projection, they become Diaporamas whether especially designed for the method or not. From here on, therefore, I shall make use of this appellation.

On the Continent, Diaporamas were welcomed with enthusiasm both in photographic and amateur cinema societies. Without in any way giving up their normal exhibitions, photo clubs added this new medium to their activities and found that it not only gave their members a new goal to work for, but drew many new spectators who eventually became participants. For the amateur cine clubs, Diaporama acted as a blood transfusion; since the boom period of the late fifties, the making of fictional or genre movies had steadily declined, and as 'club' films are rarely made any more on the Continent, because members prefer to work independently or in small groups, the average diet of monthly meetings was becoming more and more composed of holiday travelogues.

Diaporama has changed this routine, because its greater simplicity and economy, as well as the curiously poetic quality inherent in it, encourage many people to make productions based on themes that they would not or could not attempt as films. Motion pictures and Diaporamas are often presented in the same programme and to my knowledge nobody has ever objected – on the contrary, because the presence of the two media together can be quite stimulating. From a technical point of view, the Diaporamas are usually shown after the films, simply because the quality of the image (and sometimes of the sound) is superior; just as 16mm is projected after 8mm, so that the latter films will not suffer by comparison.

In Britain, club reactions were at first regrettably different, and for several years the very thought of slide-tape presentations was anathema to many of them. Letters of extraordinary virulence were penned by people who often had not even seen such programmes, proclaiming that 'no cine club can be a successful section of a still club' (or maybe it was *vice-versa*) – while on the Continent experiment had long since shown that they certainly could cohabit, and with great benefit to both. This insular attitude is fading fast, and I am glad to mention that the first major British society to adopt an understanding and open attitude to Diaporama was the one that is mistakenly thought to be the most reactionary: none other than the Royal Photographic Society itself.

The Institute of Amateur Cinematographers, with some diffidence, announced a competition for slide-tape in addition to its various film contests. Many first-class Diaporama Festivals are now organized on the Continent, and there is no doubt that the best way to improve your work in this field is by the incentive of seeing what is being done by others.

Here are a few thoughts on the subject of slide-tape competitions for Clubs who are thinking of organizing their own.

JUDGING COMPETITION ENTRIES

A slide-tape feature is a blending of image, text and music, and the judges must take into consideration the balance of these three parts, together with the rhythm of their presentation. As in a film, the unfolding of the theme is a major element, and not only is it important that it should start well, but it is essential that it should progress to an interesting conclusion.

In clubs with a long history of photographic contests, judges may find it difficult not to give priority to the technical qualities of the colour transparencies; but they must realize that, although shoddy work is not acceptable, the presentation is meant to be judged *as a whole* and that one part does not count more than another.

I have taken part in the judging of many competitions, both of photographic prints and of Diaporamas, and I believe strongly in the accuracy of the first overall impression, even though I am aware that hasty judgment is considered a sin. I see no reason why the judges should not consult together; the system whereby each one must keep to himself and note down his appreciations mathematically by attributing points to a long list of aspects both technical and artistic has always resulted, as far as I was concerned, in the most mediocre work receiving first prize, no doubt due to an averaging out of the figures.

If points must be given, I feel that they should be limited to three general headings: technique, originality and appeal. This may seem rather unbalanced, in that technique counts only for a third; but today it can be assumed that a production would not be entered in a contest unless a certain minimum standard of quality is achieved. As to my choice of the other two aspects, it does not mean that I agree entirely with some judges who consider that a subject must at all costs be novel, in the fashion of the day, and create strong reactions in the spectator. No doubt art cannot be a dull reproduction of reality, but it is not essential for a subject to be unique in order to be good; talent surely consists in producing an interesting work from a banal subject, in finding in it an aspect that nobody had noticed before, by presenting it in an original *manner.* As for strong spectator-reactions, I have in recent years unfortunately seen more than enough films and slide features in which the author's only aim seemed to be to shock the audience.

To succeed in a competition, however, a painting, photograph, song, novel, film or any type of artistic work must not only be good in itself but have some affinity with the fashion of the day; some failures cannot be explained otherwise. These productions have not suddenly become bad – it is just that they do not please the taste of the audience at that moment. I am not saying that this is right, but nothing can be done about it: adapt yourself or disappear is a law of Nature.

QUALITIES OF COMPETITION JUDGES

A good judge is hard to find and impossible to define. Great artists, great photographers or musicians are very often the worst. The least bad is probably a person of experience who, without being a specialist in the field, can at least understand the difficulties of the medium because he has tried it himself. Whenever the organizers of a contest feel obliged for reasons of prestige to call on inexperienced 'personalities' from the world of politics, 'society' or even entertainment, they can be sure that the result will be a fiasco. Municipal councillors, beauty queens or famous authors have no place here – unless they are personally interested in colour photography and sound recording and have themselves some worthwhile results to their credit.

It is difficult and not always pleasant to be a member of a judging panel, and the proclamation of the results of his deliberations can bring almost as much anguish to a judge as it does to an unlucky competitor. To criticize is not to destroy, but to enlighten. A good deal of technical progress during the last two decades can be attributed to the action of competitions and reviews in specialized journals. A contestant whose production has not been selected will curse the judges' choice for a few days, but if they have done their work correctly, he will eventually come to understand that choice and be the better for it.

VALUE OF COMPETITION TO CONTESTANTS

Emulation is necessary to the development of talent. A solitary worker cannot know how he is progressing, and club members need the incentive of an occasional competition, despite the difficulties and possibly awkward moments they may entail. The aim of a club contest is not just to provide a little publicity or an excuse for a social gathering, but to help the formation of the participating members. But on their side, the competitors must not expect miraculous results from these public judgments, and should realize that the advice given is merely a guide towards the discovery of their own personality, which only they can develop. So there are really two stages in a contest, the first being a preliminary selection carried out by the entrant himself, in his own conscience, based on his knowledge of his work and of what he has seen accomplished by his fellow members.

When sufficiently high standards are reached, the club can enter selected presentations in nationwide or international contests, and if their authors are able to participate personally in such meetings, not only will their work progress even further, but they will discover a completely new outlook. They will find that cultural and artistic media evolve in various ways according to the region or country; even identical themes may be treated in different ways.

Since France launched Diaporama festivals, other countries have joined in and participate strongly in competitions such as the one held at Epinal, whose geographical position close to the frontier has given it a European vocation. The aim of these gatherings is not to produce a standardized hotch-potch of conceptions and ideas, but on the contrary to stimulate each participant to express his own feelings and impressions in images and sound, while respecting and learning to understand the point of view expressed in the work of others.

PLANNING A SLIDE-TAPE CONTEST

There are various points to be considered by a club committee planning a slide-tape contest. For example, should there be categories, such as humour, travel, fantasy, documentary? If there is to be only one trophy, the question of subject matter cannot be raised; everything will have to be accepted, within the usual limits of 'good taste'. These limits are spreading ever wider, but for the time being one can presumably still ban pornography, politics and publicity. Without categories the selection will be more difficult, and for the judges' sake it may be preferable to envisage three smaller awards rather than one grand prize.

Technique is important. but originality should be favoured, especially if a grasp of the basic principle is shown, i.e. the choice of a subject particularly suited to slide sequences rather than to movies.

As people are apt to get carried away by slides even more than by film, it is important to impose a time limit. This not only obliges the contestant to condense his work and so produce better results, but preserves the nerves of the judges and enables them to get to bed at a reasonable hour.

Standardization of the entries is also essential, in order to simplify the task of the projectionist who, at least during the preliminary judging, will not be the author. For the same reason, they must be accompanied by a booklet giving all the necessary projection indications.

The slides should be glass-mounted, for protection and because popping in and out of focus can ruin the presentation, especially with dual-projection. Many festivals and contests still insist on a tape speed of 7½ ips but the quality of 3¾ ips is now so good that there is really no reason for not permitting the use of the slower speed. A synchronizing pulse naturally makes for easier and more accurate projection, but its use depends on the facilities available to the contestants and on the equipment that will be employed at the time of the presentations.

Based on these points, here are some general rules for a competition. I have omitted giving details of entrance forms, packaging, return postage, etc., which are obviously the same as for film or photo contests.

GENERAL RULES FOR A SLIDE-TAPE CONTEST

The following specimen rules are largely similar to those usually applied in Diaporama festivals.

1. Entries must consist of:
   (a) A series of slides.
   (b) A magnetic tape.
   (c) Written text and necessary indications for projection.
2. *The duration* of each series must not exceed 12 min.
3. *The slides:*
   All sizes up to and including super-slides, but preferably 35mm. Outside measurements of mount in all cases to be

2 × 2 in. Must be mounted under glass, in mounts to fit standard projectors.

Each slide must be marked with identification of the series, the sequence number in that series, and a red dot in the upper right-hand corner, facing the projectionist.

The sequence should have an introductory and an end title, and may include 'presents' and other titles if desired. The quantity of the slides is up to the contestant, but a minimum of 8 sec screen time per slide can be considered necessary.

Trick effects such as the sandwiching of two slides in the same mount are accepted, but the actual images must have been obtained by photographic means, either on a colour or a monochrome emulsion.

4. *The tape:*

Should be recorded at 7½ ips (acceptance of 3¾ ips is up to the individual club). It must be in one continuous band (no turning over).

The recording should begin with the spoken title and the author's name, followed by the numbers 5,4,3,2,1,0. Then begins the actual sequence.

Generally monaural only, although some competitions now accept stereo tracks. If a four-track tape is used for a monaural production, the track beneath the one being used must be blank, so that the tape may eventually be played on a twin-track machine.

5. *The text:*

In order to make accurate projection possible, a booklet giving all necessary indications must accompany the entries. It should include:

(a) The sequence number of the slides with a brief description of each.
(b) The timing.
(c) The written text, laid out in a clear manner opposite the corresponding slide.
(d) If necessary, indications concerning rapid and slow passage or other effects of transition from one picture to the next.

The booklet should enable a projectionist unfamiliar with the production to present it without error.

6. The presence of the author or of his representative is authorized and even recommended in the case of productions

which require complex visual effects or very precise synchronization.

HINTS FOR THE CONTESTANT

Apart from the general advice already given there are three basic rules for contestants in slide-tape competitions.

1. Make sure the glass of your slide-mounts is clean and dust-free.
2. Record your tape at a sufficiently high level. An increase in volume to enable it to be heard in a large hall also increases the background noise.
3. Although accidental erasure is very rare, it is wise to keep a copy of the tape.

Advanced Techniques

In recent years, the more ambitious producers of slide-tape features have not only taken advantage of dual projection but have widened the scope and impact of their presentations by using more than one screen. Some modern 'spectaculars' are so complex and involve such a multitude of electronic equipment that even a summary description of their technique would be beyond the scope of this book. However, a triple-screen production with a simplified form of stereophonic sound is well within the possibilities of an enthusiastic group of members of a photographic or amateur cinema club.

TRIPLE SCREEN

Although experiments in this medium have been going on since the dawn of the magic lantern, the two key dates in triple-screen presentation and stereophony (as applied to cinema) are 1927 and 1951. For the original silent version of his celebrated *Napoleon,* Abel Gance had already enlarged certain sequences, notably of the departure of the Army for Italy, by means of a 'triptych'. Fred Waller, who had been experimenting with triple-projection as a means of flight simulation for the training of pilots during World War II, commercialized the system in the 'fifties under the name of *Cinerama.* Its most notable feature was the gigantic curved screen, so concave that its outside edges almost touched the front row of the stalls. Because of this, the beams of the three projectors installed in the balcony crossed each other, the right-hand machine projecting on the left side of the screen and *vice-versa.* With the relatively flat screens used for slide presentations this is not necessary, and the images are lined up side by side in the same order as the projectors showing them.

The first performances of this system translated into terms of still colour photography were given in Europe by Kodak-Pathé of Paris, who had already pioneered public shows of dual slide projection on a single screen, and since then their 'spectaculars in colour' have been acclaimed in other parts of the world. At the 1969 New York Photo Expo, for example, two of their teams presented a number of such shows which were exceptionally well received. It is interesting to note that they did not use synchronizers. The operators took their cues for the changeovers from the soundtrack, and made them manually. These presentations are put on with six projectors grouped in three pairs, each with a changeover unit. There can be one very wide panoramic screen, or more usually three screens are placed side by side. The latter system is more practical, enabling easier setting up and transportation.

In preparing a show of this type, the first important decision to take is the format of the slides. If the horizontal 35mm frame is maintained, a triple screen will have a 'letter box' proportion of $4\frac{1}{2} \times 1$.

Square slides approximate the original Cinerama format of 3×1.

An unusual arrangement was adopted by Agfa-Gevaert for certain presentations: it would seem to make use of the 'Rapid' 1 in. square film size in the centre, and half-frame vertically at each side.

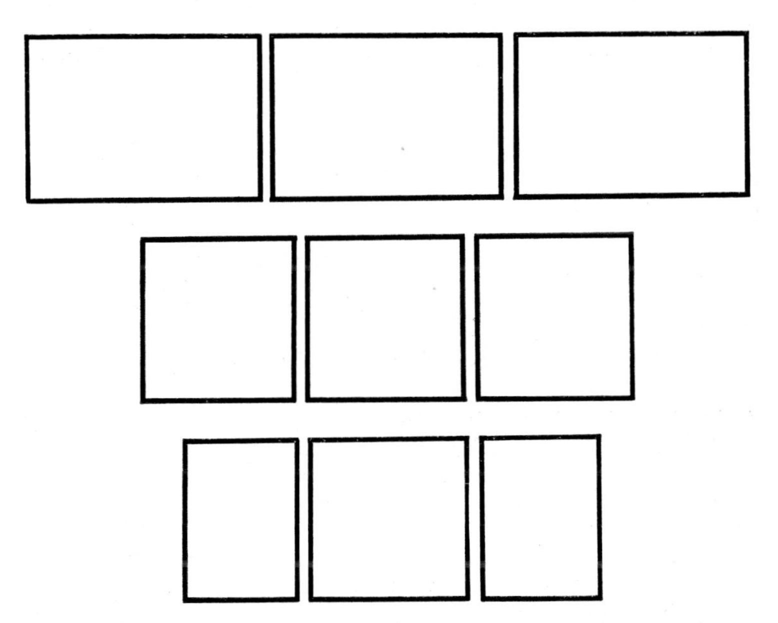

Various formats of triple-screen presentation.

SHOOTING PANORAMIC VIEWS

When it is desired to form one single continuous view of a landscape from the three images, the same technique has to be used as in the making of a panoramic montage on paper; but even greater precaution in lining up the horizon is necessary, because prints can be trimmed, whereas slides are projected in their entirety.

To ensure that all the pictures are taken from the same viewpoint, the camera must be mounted on a tripod with a rotating head. Ideally, it should turn about the front nodal point of the lens (just behind its front element) but the normal arrangement usually gives good results. It is vital that the installation be absolutely level, otherwise the horizon will not be straight across the picture, but will curve down at the sides if the camera was pointing up, and *vice-versa.*

Some tripod heads are specially designed for taking panoramas. They swivel around a fixed base graduated in degrees and have a built-in spirit-level. With a normal tripod, the lining up of the images must be done visually, by noting a feature of the landscape on the extreme edge of the frame. If you are shooting from left to right, you line up the right-hand side of the first of the three pictures with a tree or building, then swivel the camera so that this pointer is on the left of the viewfinder. Then you choose another guidemark on the right side, and swivel again until it is lined up on the left.

An imaginary view of the Paris skyline, as it might be seen from the heights of Montmartre. The tripod not being absolutely horizontal, the camera was pointing downwards; as a result, the side pictures are not level with the one in the centre.

There is plenty of subject matter for panoramas: city skylines, mountain ranges, landscapes with rivers – preferably with plenty of variety in their silhouettes, as a flat unbroken horizon is rather boring unless there is a specific reason for it, such as exploration of 'limitless deserts'.

Take care that the same moving object does not appear in two sections of a landscape! During the unavoidable time-lapse between exposures, it may have passed from one slide to the next. And on windy days, the cloud formations may not match up too well. However, this latter defect is not as critical as in a printed photographic montage, because triple-screen slide presentations do not pretend to be one continuous image, in fact they look rather better if a narrow black band separates one screen from the other.

COMBINING THE PICTURES

A single panorama spread across the three screens can be very striking, but this is not the real purpose of the method. If it were, a more accurate line-up without gaps could be obtained by making use of a single camera and projector fitted with anamorphic (CinemaScope) lenses, or by taking the photographs with a special panoramic camera. The main idea of the set-up is to enable different pictures to be presented simultaneously, juxtaposing similarities or contrasts for visual effect.

Although the smoothest presentation is naturally obtained by dual projection on to each screen, it is not always possible to gather

The Paris skyline in three sections for a triple-screen presentation.

The side panels only have changed. L.S. of Notre-Dame replaced by C.U. of a pair of its celebrated monsters; L.S. of Arc de Triomphe by C.U. of one of its sculptures. Note that both these shots are composed so as to face inwards.

together six similar projectors and three changeover units (or alternatively three special dual machines). Three single projectors can give interesting results, although the blacking out between slides soon becomes tiring to the eyes when taking place in three places at once. An acceptable compromise is to make use of four projectors: two linked together with a changeover unit for dissolves on the central panel, and a single projector with normal slide-changing on each side. In this case, the spectacle may be designed to concentrate mainly on the centre, the side panels being an accompaniment.

Whichever system is adopted, considerable planning and rehearsal are necessary, particularly as the tape recording is likely to be as complicated to prepare as the visuals. Stereophonic sound may be unnecessary in the general run of single-screen slide shows, but with multiple-projection spectaculars it really comes into its own.

STEREOPHONIC SOUND

We have two ears for the same reason that we have two eyes: to enable us to judge direction and distance. Sound waves travel at a fixed rate of speed, and a sound located to the left of us reaches our left ear a fraction of a second before it arrives at the right one. This time-difference is noted by our brain, which automatically interprets it into terms of direction. However excellent the recording of a range of sounds may be – and nowadays the fidelity is very high indeed – this dimensional quality is lost if it emerges from one loudspeaker only.

In theory, a perfect method for the reproducton of spatial positioning would be to place two microphones from 6 to 8 in. apart (the distance between human ears), keep separated the signals picked up by each, and listen to the result on headphones. This technique of binaural sound (for two ears) is obviously not very practical; and if the headphones are replaced by loudspeakers also a few inches apart, each ear then hears the output of both almost simultaneously and cannot distinguish between them.

To solve this problem, engineers arbitrarily enlarge the spacing to 5, 10, 20 ft or more, and increase the gap between microphones accordingly. The result is an exaggerated effect of sound-separation sometimes called 'ping-pong', which is a source of great delight to stereo enthusiasts but is disapproved by many leading musicians who rightly consider that a feeling of *presence* requires 'ambience' (a certain reverberation from the surrounding walls of a concert hall) and 'depth' (levels of sound that appear to be behind or in front of others – a distinction obtainable with a single track) even more than side to side movement. Multi-channel recording and other complicated techniques are being developed to reproduce all the subtleties of tone heard by an orchestral conductor on his podium. But I think we shall be forgiven if we consider that our aim is *entertainment* and not musical perfection, and so adhere to the 'ping-pong' school by making our sounds follow our images as they move about the screen.

Professional motion-picture stereophony uses four or six tracks, numerous speakers behind the screen and a circuit of loudspeakers in the auditorium. Amateur technique disposes of twin tracks and a speaker at each end of the screen, the 'centre' being obtained by careful balancing of the recording.

PERSPECTA SOUND

The above remarks apply to 'true' stereo, recorded on separate tracks, and on playback distributed automatically to the speakers via two or more amplifiers. But there is also a form of artificial stereo which is produced by passing the sound from one speaker to another by switching. Known as Perspecta sound, it was developed to enable old movies with optical tracks to be re-issued. The standard single track was still used, but a controlling device channelled it towards one of three loudspeakers located in the centre and to right and left of the screen.

This simple system is of particular interest to amateurs, because it enables additional loudspeakers to be placed either behind the screen or in the body of the hall while still retaining a standard twin track. At strategic moments the sound from one of the tracks is diverted from its usual speaker to another. If applied in reasonable doses, it is quite possible to do this manually during the show.

RECORDING A STEREO TRACK

Although the basic principles are the same for both monaural and stereophonic recording, the latter requires not only more complex equipment but very precise planning with regard to the positioning of the various sound elements. From an aesthetic point of view, this requires answers to certain preliminary questions: Will the text be heard from the centre of the screen, or should it be spoken by two narrators answering each other from either side? Will the music be merely transcribed from a stereo disc and played back in a normal manner through both speakers, or will it be made to move around and about?

Unless the feature is an animated and lively fantasy, stereo effects should be used with even greater moderation than visual effects, because they can soon become more of a distraction than an improvement. It is tempting to play them to the full; but just as the best slides are not necessarily those that include every colour of the rainbow, so an overdose of stereophonic trickery can appear more suited to a funfair than to a serious presentation.

For the actual taping, the stereo recorder should have several input plugs, preferably all mixable and with the possibility of varying the intensity on both channels. If there is to be any re-recording, two stereo machines are normally necessary, although a certain amount can be done with the help of one additional monaural recorder.

With the standard two speakers placed one at each end of the screens, the positioning of the sound is fairly limited:

TEXT ON ONE SIDE, MUSIC AND EFFECTS ON THE OTHER

A monaural microphone is connected to one track, a monaural record player to the other. This is really basic, and rather absurd. The only advantage of the method over straightforward single-track presentation is that as the music and effects track is detached from the commentary, its volume need not be manipulated quite so much during the recording.

NARRATION IN THE CENTRE

Obtained either by means of a monaural microphone with a special dual connection, or a stereo microphone, balanced equally between the two tracks.

DIALOGUE BETWEEN TWO NARRATORS

This solution is more interesting. A microphone is connected to one track for the first narrator, and a separate microphone to the second track for the other. The microphones must be highly directional and record only their particular voice.

SOUND EFFECTS

To lovers of ping-pong effects, nothing can equal the thrill of hearing a horse galloping across the room or that old steam locomotive coming down the line. The magic works even more when synchronized to a trio of pictures appearing successively from side to side of the screens. If the sound effect is produced 'live', the obvious way to record it is to place the two directional microphones at a short distance from each other, then begin the effect in front of the first and move progressively towards the second. The speed of the advance is calculated according to the changing of the screen images.

If on the other hand the sound effect has been previously recorded on monaural disc or tape, the record player or second recorder is connected to both inputs of the stereo machine. The re-recording starts on the first track, the volume of which is then lowered while that of the second track is raised until it takes over completely.

MUSIC

With stereo discs, the twin outputs of the pick-up are linked normally to the two tracks, the recording level being balanced between the two. If a separate control is available for each track, it is possible to exaggerate certain effects, such as one musical instrument answering another.

MULTI-SCREEN AUTOMATIC AUDIO-VISUAL DISPLAYS

It took some time to catch on, but now that slide-tape has been accepted, there is apparently no limit to the different ways which imaginative producers are finding to present it in a spectacular manner.

For example, in France a night programme in aid of nature preservation was given in a game reserve, where 45 giant screens had been placed along the main pathway. On to them were projected transparencies of animals and birds as well as reproductions from paintings and illuminated manuscripts concerning wild-life. As visitors strolled from one screen to another, loudspeakers set in the trees played recordings of cries and birdsong taped in various parts of the world.

In Britain, a circular theatre was installed at an *Ideal Homes Exhibition* in which 40 projectors, set up in pairs, were used to project a succession of images (some changing rapidly from one to the other and others dissolving) on to twenty screens in juxtaposition placed at a fairly high level around the inside periphery of the enclosure. In some commercial displays, small screens are arranged into designs and the slides projected on to them from behind. These change rapidly, and from being completely different, they can build up into one impressive picture over all the screens at once. 'Multi-media' fashion shows in theatrical style may incorporate slide projection, live dancers, stereo sound and lighting effects.

The scripting, photography and recording of lavish productions such as these call for both time and money and, as the most costly component is the human element, the presentations are mechanized by means of very sophisticated electronic control systems.

The ultimate in giant presentation is being planned in France. The screens are to be several thousand feet high – yet are bound to be as dazzlingly white as driven snow, because the transparencies will be projected directly on to the sides of the Alps!

Having reached this summit, there is nothing more to be said, except perhaps that in the medium of slide-tape features, the sky is now the limit.

Example of Slide-tape Feature

Statues in a park don't move, so one could say that the subject of *Standing Room Only* is perfect for slide-tape. It could have been used for a film, but it would have been more expensive and technically much more complicated. I consider that slides did the job far better.

This is a relatively slow production: there are 46 pictures for a running-time of 12 min. Visually it is a straightforward series of transparencies with only one or two planned effects (which are not essential) and so would be suitable for presentation with a single projector.

The soundtrack is more complex, and the three sequences reproduced here have been selected to show the different styles adopted in its making. It required three narrators (the two interpreting the roles of statues have French accents, which contribute a great deal to the atmosphere of the feature) music, sound effects and at one point an echo-chamber.

Projection is very simple, even 'by ear' without a synchronizer, because the commentary is almost continuous and mainly of the one-picture, one-phrase type; the exceptions to this being some short sections of music only, and one or two slide-changes during the course of a sentence.

Opening title music (small jazz combination).
Music fades down behind voice. First narrator (male):

This rather odd-looking wall forms one of the boundaries of the park of Fontainebleau palace. I came to know it well, for there was a time when I used to pass along here nearly every day.

I still don't know what all these statues represent, or who put them there, or why; in a way I prefer not to know because I have a feeling that such cold facts would remove their curious appeal. I like to think that they just came together by themselves.

There are so many statues in French parks that one barely notices them; but these are different. I saw them so often that after a while we became friends, and I began to imagine that they had a life of their own. A rather dull, even uncomfortable life, filled with regrets and dreams that were unfulfilled.

It was this one who first aroused my pity. Far away across that still water, cut off from the others, she looked lost and lonely. And at the same time she seemed so shy.

– peering dubiously out of her niche as though she hardly dared to enquire what was going on above her head. To make it worse, if she did look up, a stern-looking woman across the way was constantly staring at her.

Second narrator (middle-aged woman, sounding cross):
What do you mean, staring at her? I look at her from time to time because she seems rather nice, and I'm sorry that she's too far off to speak to without shouting, which would not be polite. . . . She is no doubt a more agreeable person than some of those who surround me up here. But one cannot choose one's neighbours. . . .

Here I am, exposed to all dangers, with a child to look after; and I don't feel that anyone out of this group would be of use, in case of trouble.

That couple there wouldn't be much help. They may be quite pleasant to know, but they only have eyes for each other; and she's so clumsy, always dropping things. They completely ignore me and everything around them.

So I like to keep my eyes open, which is not a matter of staring, as you put it, but of taking my responsibilities. Our situation is not an easy one, and like everybody these days, we have our problems and difficulties.

For instance, have you tried standing still all day on one leg? The ancient Egyptians understood comfort; in those days we statues had both feet planted firmly on the ground. But when we arrived here, it had been decreed that no line of grace or beauty could be straight, and we are condemned to be on our toes for ever.

The following short sequence of bent legs and feet is accompanied by music only. By the same group as the title music, it contains rather odd-sounding creaks that might be imagined to come from rheumaticky limbs.

This opening sequence was easy to record. But the next extract, which comes towards the end of the production, was more involved. We begin it on the last shot of a sequence commentated by the original narrator.

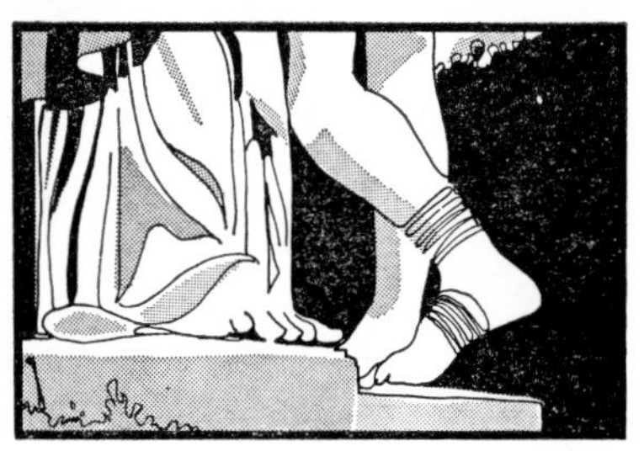

. . . This poor lady looks rather scared – I think it's because of that fierce Roman half-hidden behind the trees. . . .

Brief trumpet fanfare, followed immediately by third narrator (very deep male voice). His text begins in an echoing effect, which gradually disappears.

Ho! Ho! So the poor girl is frightened of me! She need not worry. I am not at all interested in her . . . or in any of those other sad creatures, always sighing and sorry for themselves!

In my day, in Rome, our women were strong and noble. Our towns knew how to honour them in stone . . . but everything then was designed for Eternity and in harmony with Nature.

These men of today can keep their parks, their gardens. . . . Just give me a field of poppies like the one near the cenotaph our great Augustus had built in honour of his nephews at Glanum.

The thought of those wonderful times brings them all back to me . . . (*mix in crowd noises that continue in background*) the theatre, the crowds shouting and laughing, the fanfares . (*sound of fanfares, added to crowd noises*)

. and towering above them all, the one, the great Augustus. There was a statue. Vibrant with life – a man, yes, but an emperor – and also a god!

(*Fade out crowd and fanfares; short silence*)

And I, who have known such splendour, remain here, among these fools – fools. . . . I despise them all!

(*Echoing effect begins again on 'among these fools' and increases to crescendo.*)

This short sunset sequence which ends *Standing Room Only* is accompanied by the final part of an orchestral rendering of Debussy's *Clair de Lune* and fades out with the music.

The rhythm of this last series of slides is very calm, and they are linked by slow dissolves. The major part of the production is presented with normal-speed mixes; shot number 7 appears in a rapid 'cut' on the words 'What do you mean, staring at her?' Instant change-over is also used between the shots of the 'bent legs' sequence (12–15).

The only visual trick effects are at the beginning and end of the Roman sequence. It will be noted that the bust is shown against a black background of trees. As the flashback to the past begins, the statue of the Roman lady appears in the dark right-hand section, and this double image is held for a moment before the martial 'narrator' fades out. The reverse effect is employed at the close of the sequence: the statue of Augustus remains visible for a few seconds by the side of the bust.

The two slides of the bust were composed – one on the left, the other to the right of the frame – with these effects in mind, the statues of the Roman matron and of Augustus having been taken some time previously during a trip to Provence, the former at Vaison-la-Romaine and the latter in the Antique Theatre at Orange.

Index

Numbers in *italics* refer to illustrations